A SOCIETY UNDER STRESS

Children and Young People in Northern Ireland

A Society under Stress

Children and Young People in Northern Ireland

Jeremy and Joan Harbison

Open Books

First published in 1980 by Open Books Publishing Ltd
West Compton House, Nr Shepton Mallet, Somerset, England

ISBN 0 7291 0128 2

Text set in 10/11 pt IBM Press Roman, printed and bound in
Great Britain at The Pitman Press, Bath

To Janet and all the children
living in a society
under stress

Contents

List of contributors

Halla Beloff — Senior Lecturer, Department of Psychology, University of Edinburgh

Frederick W. Boal — Senior Lecturer, Department of Geography, Queen's University of Belfast

Brendan Bunting — Postgraduate Student, Department of Psychology, New University of Ulster

Ed Cairns — Lecturer, Department of Psychology, New University of Ulster

Norman Caven — Deputy, Social Research Division, Central Economic Service, Department of Finance (N.I.)

Bob Cormack — Lecturer in Sociology, Department of Social Studies, Queen's University of Belfast

J. Damian Curran — Senior Psychologist, Northern Ireland Training Schools

Ruth Elliott — Senior Clinical Psychologist, Department of Mental Health, Belfast City Hospital

Frank Fee — Principal Educational Psychologist, Belfast Education and Library Board

Jeremy J. M. Harbison — Social Research Division, Central Economic Service, Department of Finance (N.I.)

Joan I. Harbison — Senior Lecturer in Education, Stranmillis College of Education, Belfast

Ken Heskin — Lecturer, Department of Psychology, Trinity College, Dublin

Edgar F. Jardine — Headmaster, Assessment Unit, Rathgael Training School, Bangor, Co Down

William H. Lockhart — Senior Psychologist, Northern Ireland Regional Assessment Centre

James McKernan — Research Officer, Northern Ireland Council for Educational Research, Queen's University of Belfast

G. William Mercer — Lecturer, Psychology Department, Cape Breton College, Canada

Russell C. Murray   Research Fellow, Institute of Population Studies, University of Exeter

Bob Osborne   Lecturer in Social Policy, School of Sociology and Social Policy, Ulster Polytechnic

Willie Thompson   Lecturer in Education, Department of Further Professional Studies in Education, Queen's University of Belfast

Jean Whyte   Research Fellow, Institute of Irish Studies, Queen's University of Belfast

John A. Wilson   Director, Research Unit of the Northern Ireland Council for Educational Research, Queen's University of Belfast

Preface

During the last ten years Northern Ireland has become an all too familiar news item for most of the population of the United Kingdom and for many others further afield. While much has been written and said on the subject of events within this small province little serious scientific investigation has been carried out into the causes, effects or implications of those events; in particular psychologists have been noticeable only by their absence. The apparent lack of involvement by this professional discipline is all the more surprising since particular concern has been expressed by many on the position of children and young people in Northern Ireland and the inter-active influence between them and their environment.

With this anxiety concerning children and young people very much in mind the Northern Ireland Regional Office of the British Psychological Society sponsored a two-day conference in September 1978 on young people living in the present environment of Northern Ireland in an attempt to give impetus to current research and to stimulate and encourage further projects. This book is one of the results of that conference, although it contains material not presented there and omits some which was. Most of the contributors have a psychological background but a number of other disciplines are represented. This reflects the concern of professionals working with young people in the province, as did the wide variety of professions represented amongst the delegates at the conference. It was this cross-disciplinary professional response to the conference that suggested that a more permanent record of the available research and conclusions was necessary. We hope that this book will provide that record and prove useful to all those interested in the development of young people.

We have received a great deal of help from a number of people in the preparation of the book and we should like to record our particular thanks to all the contributors who met our demands and deadlines with great efficiency. A very special debt of gratitude is due to David Hale for his conference organisation and constant help and support before, during and after the conference. Finally we must thank Miss G.

Casement for her careful typing, her cheerfulness in face of all our demands and her unfailing optimism, and Patrick Taylor for his co-operation and continuing encouragement throughout the preparation of the book.

Jeremy J. M. Harbison
Joan I. Harbison
Belfast 1979

SECTION I
SETTING THE SCENE

1

'Unless you're from the place you can't start to understand it'?

Joan I. Harbison and Jeremy J. M. Harbison

Darby (1976) has recently listed seven hundred publications on Northern Ireland and this only took him to mid-1975. Since then, as Whyte (1978) has pointed out 'the stream of publication has poured remorselessly on' (p. 257). It would seem that all that needs to be said should have already been said and not only the sceptic might seek the justification for yet another book. One answer is indicated in the next chapter's critical research review of the available studies of children and young people in Northern Ireland which finds them seriously deficient from a methodological view point. This conclusion was also reached by Taylor and Nelson (1978) in their conference review for *The Trouble with Being Young*. They noted the absence of relevant hard data and 'perception' studies which might challenge a number of unsubstantiated assumptions about young people in Northern Ireland and the areas of research which have been neglected or inadequately explored.

The plethora of articles has led to little increase in understanding of either the 'Northern Ireland problem' in general or the particular effects and influences the experience has had and may be having on the people who live in the province. A detailed reading of current publications may in fact lead one to the view that there is an increasing realisation that simple answers, or commonsense views, are frequently inadequate or simply wrong within the particular Northern Ireland situation.

It is all too easy to catalogue the dire social, economic and political problems which exist in the province. Social and economic conditions are amongst the worst in the E.E.C.; Northern Ireland has been described by *The Times* as having the 'worst housing in Europe', with one in five of its houses defined (by the Housing Executive) as unfit for habitation; poverty (and particularly family poverty) is greater than in any other region of the United Kingdom through a combination of large families, high prices (particularly for fuel), and low earnings. The present unemployment rate of 14 per cent is double the U.K. rate and in certain areas rises much above this.

Infant mortality is higher than even the distressing U.K. average and other indices of health and well-being, such as the incidence of alcoholism, are similarly unsatisfactory. For young people the statistics indicate an equally discouraging situation: the juvenile unemployment rate has risen by almost 300 per cent in the five years up to 1977 and school leavers have generally poorer educational qualifications than in England and Wales (*Opportunities at Sixteen*, 1978). The picture relating to violence is, of course, widely known: in the last ten years almost 2,000 people have died as a result of violence; by the middle of 1978 approaching £300 million had been paid in compensation for property damage or personal injury; the rate of involvement of young people in grave offences in Northern Ireland, expressed as a proportion of the total juvenile population, is approximately thirteen times the rate for England and Wales and, for children under the age of eighteen convicted of murder, the rate is twenty-two times that for England and Wales (Millham et al., 1978). This and other information is reported in greater detail in later chapters; suffice it to say here that there exists for young people in Northern Ireland an appalling combination of circumstances, both social and economic, which inevitably influences the way people feel, perceive and react.

There is however another, less well recognised face of Northern Ireland. Whilst social conditions are undoubtedly bad, social behaviour differs significantly in a variety of ways from the rest of Britain. Marriage stability is high and in general family cohesion and support is greater than in other industrialised communities. A recent report (Rogers and Titterington, 1978) concludes, after an examination of child abuse through Health Board registers, that 'reported cases of incidents of child abuse are considerably less than would be expected from the estimate of the national figures'. In spite of the traditional view of the Irish being frequent and heavy drinkers, studies show that average N.I. households spend less on alcohol than their U.K. counterparts (*Family Expenditure Survey*, 1977) and that three times as many adults are complete abstainers than is the case elsewhere (Blaney and McKenzie, 1978). More young people stay on voluntarily at school after the statutory leaving age. In 1976 over 33 per cent of sixteen-year-olds stayed at school in Northern Ireland while only 28 per cent did so in England and Wales. At eighteen years of age the proportions were 9.4 as against 6.8 per cent. A greater percentage of pupils achieve 'A' level success and more go from school to full-time further and higher education than is the case in England and Wales (*Opportunities at Sixteen*, 1978). Even within the context of crime the picture is not quite so 'obvious' as it might appear. Whilst the numbers of crimes known to the police in Northern Ireland have jumped by almost 150 per cent since 1968, there are still considerably fewer offences per

thousand population in the province than in England and Wales (26 per
thousand in N.I., 43 per thousand in England and Wales in 1976). A
similar situation prevails with juveniles. The latest official figures
(1978) show that proportionately, N.I. has only half as many juveniles
found guilty of both indictable and other offences as is the case in
England and Wales. Indeed one author (Leyton, 1974) was forced to
ask not why so many people have died in the years of trouble, rather
why so *few* have been killed. The rate of murder is, he pointed out,
much less than the normal murder rate in Detroit. In spite of the widespread categorisation of the situation as one of 'civil war', one must
ask why there have not been large-scale clashes between the population
groups. Finally, while assassinations have taken place, only a tiny
proportion occurred in the countryside where such assassinations
would be relatively easy.

The available studies, reports, articles and books do little to help the
understanding of these paradoxes. In a number of areas basic descriptive
information is still lacking, and acceptable or adequate theories on the
sources of conflict are scarce. Even more important, there has been a
paucity of studies which even attempt to document the effects that a
decade of disturbance could have had on the population of the
province, and in particular on the young people. The few studies
presently available in print suffer from methodological defects and
inadequacies, as later chapters will indicate.

However there is some evidence of the development of a more
positive approach. Whyte (1978) has recently discussed and evaluated
the various theories which have been put forward to account for
Northern Ireland's problems. His article suggests potentially interesting
and valuable areas where research might be directed, and it is provo-
cative in that he concludes: 'Anyone who studies the Ulster conflict
must be struck by the intensity of feeling. It seems to go beyond what
is required by a rational defence of the divergent interests which
undoubtedly exist. There is an irrational element here, a welling of deep
unconscious forces, which can only be explained by an appeal to
social psychology.' (p. 278)

Informed critics have also turned their attention to the needs and
problems of academic research (Taylor and Nelson, 1978). Not only are
the limitations of previous work exposed, but further suggestions are
being made about the directions future research might follow. The
inadequacies of present information are at last being remedied. Both
government and statutory agencies have initiated and subsequently
published quantitative material which greatly facilitates the appreciation of the social, physical and economic problems facing the
community. Examples must include the detailed *Areas of Special Social
Need* (1976) report which quantified the multiple disadvantages

experienced by large numbers of people within the greater Belfast area, the Housing Executive *House Condition Survey* (1974) and *Household Survey* (1975) which documented the physical housing problems across Northern Ireland and the extent and types of stress facing households in the province. Academic workers and pressure groups have also produced basic descriptive material. Notable here are the two Child Poverty Action Group reports on poverty and family poverty in Northern Ireland (Evason, 1976, 1978), and Boal's pioneering work on social malaise in Belfast (1974). Other recent work has described the effects of violence on social and public services and the responses these services have made to the challenges presented (Darby and Williamson, 1978).

It is against this background that the present volume has been produced and it is hoped that the material presented will extend the positive role of research by making available a wide range of recently reported research studies, few of which are easily available elsewhere. The subject matter has been restricted to children and young people, with an age range of pre-school to late teens. This restriction is deliberate. Not only are these the groups around which most anxiety revolves concerning the effects of the present situation, but psychologists have greater experience and knowledge of the factors involved in the development of young people.

The book has a number of additional aims to that of making available recent objective research on children and young people. It is hoped that it will have a heuristic value, and that the material will have a role to play in challenging other workers to examine, extend and if necessary demolish the present views. Traditional experimental approaches may have limitations within a dynamic conflict situation such as presently exists; present experience should lead to the development of more adaptive and flexible methodology.

Above all, however, description and understanding are only valuable if they lead to a constructive response stategy by individuals and professional groups, or to a modification in policy by agencies or government. Research within an applied framework is only justified if it is directed at change for the better in the person, in the environment, or in the structures which determine and influence so much behaviour.

The volume is in six sections. These include a research review, descriptive studies of the behaviour of young people, the changes in their environment, and their perception of and aspirations for their future. A major potential medium for change must be the school and the educational system: section 3 describes potential and practical possibilities for utilising education as a major change agent. A later section examines particular groups of young people who are either 'at risk' or who have already come into contact with the law, and changes

which can occur as a result of a brief period of imposed intervention.
Experimental studies on the development of attitudes, ethnic perceptions and values of children and young people in the province are
reported in section 5. The final chapter is a review of the research
presented and its implications for Northern Ireland and beyond, with
suggestions for future directions and methods of research in the
province.

Finally, it may be of interest to note that all the research reported in
this book has been completed by professional workers operating within
Northern Ireland; the initial review is written by an Ulsterman living in
the Republic of Ireland and the epilogue is the work of an academic
who spent a considerable proportion of her working life teaching
within Northern Ireland. Whilst being 'born and bred' in Northern
Ireland cannot be a justification for producing this book, it at least
answers one oft-repeated retort to academic research on the province
that 'unless you're from the place you can't start to understand it!'

2

Children and young people in Northern Ireland: a research review

Ken Heskin

Major contributions to the comprehension of Northern Ireland's problems have been made by historians, geographers, social administrators, political scientists, sociologists and journalists. Psychologists have not been in the vanguard of reasoned and disciplined thought on the problems of life in Ulster, although it is fair to add that the conference from which this publication springs marks a turning point in that state of affairs.

In a way, this tardiness is puzzling, for in Northern Ireland there exist some classic examples of problems which have engaged psychologists for most of this century. There are problems of attitudes, attitude formation and attitude change; problems of group identity, group allegiance and inter-group conflict; problems of stereotyping, prejudice and communication.

Perhaps psychologists in Northern Ireland have been intimidated by their appreciation of the complexity of the situation viewed from a vantage point, or perhaps a disadvantage point, of local knowledge and experience? As the man said, 'Anyone who isn't confused here doesn't know what's going on'. Yet, the range of disciplines which can, and have, yielded important perspectives on the peculiar dynamics of Northern Irish society is wide and it seems unlikely that a mere acquaintance with the complexities of Northern Irish society has prevented psychologists in particular from airing their views. Certainly, such restraint does not normally characterise their behaviour.

A second possibility is that psychologists have been discouraged by the regrettably simple-minded nature of some early work carried out under the mantle of psychology. Dr Rona Fields' (1973, 1977) missionary descent has provided a warning against the twin dangers of allowing personal prejudices to ride roughshod over a discipline and of allowing the theoretical flotsam and jetsam of a discipline to wander capriciously over dubious data.

Reporting Dr Fields' work in the *Times Educational Supplement* of 9 February 1973, Sue Cameron was given to believe that 'A simple exercise like making a papier mâché farm taught them [i.e. the kids] to work together to make materials. They began to learn to share and at the same time take pride in individual work without competitive pressure'. This poses the interesting idea that the answer to the problems of Northern Ireland's future citizens lies in persuading Readymix to switch production from concrete to papier mâché, the resultant product to be dolloped round the province under the supervision and direction of Dr Fields. Be that as it may, this sort of work did not blaze an attractive trail for other psychologists to follow.

However, before going on to consider more valuable research into the problems of Northern Irish youth, it would be appropriate to look briefly at some of the 'bald facts' of stress in Northern Ireland.

The July 1978 figures for unemployment in Northern Ireland show that 13.4 per cent of the work force is unemployed, compared to 6.6 per cent in the rest of the United Kingdom. This is the highest figure since 1938, yet it conceals unemployment rates of hair-raising proportions in certain areas of the province and in certain areas of the city of Belfast, as studies by the Queen's University Department of Geography and others indicate (Boal, Doherty and Pringle, 1974). Within this context, the prospects for young school-leavers seeking employment are bleak, especially for those without formal qualifications.

Compounding the problem of unemployment is the fact that wages in the province are on average only 86 per cent of wages in Great Britain based on 1974 data (*Regional Statistics*, No.11, 1975) and the province has proportionately twice as many people as Great Britain on very low pay, again based on 1974 figures and using £30 per week as the standard. To gild the economic lily, prices, apart from housing, are generally higher in Northern Ireland than elsewhere in the U.K. and even the cost of housing has increased sharply towards the G.B. level in recent years.

The combination of these circumstances, plus the fact that Northern Irish families tend to be larger than families in Great Britain, has led to the situation that while N.I. contains only 2.8 per cent of the total U.K. population, it receives 11.4 per cent of all payments made to supplement the earnings of low-income families where the head of the household is in full-time employment. Evason, in her 1976 booklet entitled *Poverty: The Facts in Northern Ireland,* points out that while family size is a more important factor in producing reliance on Family Income Supplement in N.I. than Great Britain, low wages are a more important factor than large families in Northern Ireland. This judgement hinges on precisely what definition of 'large family' one chooses to make, but 30 per cent of N.I. claimants have two or less children, 47 per cent

three or less children, and 65 per cent four or less children. Evason
(1976) estimates that, in all, nearly 200,000 children under sixteen in
Northern Ireland, that is to say almost 40 per cent of all children, are
being brought up in families with resources below the official needs
level.

What sort of housing do Northern Ireland's children have to grow up
in? In 1970, Evason notes, 33 per cent of dwellings in the province had
been built before 1881, 15 per cent had been erected between 1921 and
1941, and 40 per cent were built in the post-war period, much of the
latter being worst of all from the point of view of public amenities,
community development and standard of design and construction.

The Housing Condition Survey conducted by the N.I. Housing
Executive in 1974 found that 19.6 per cent of the housing stock in the
province (almost 90,000 dwellings) was unfit for habitation; the
comparable 1971 British figure was 7.3 per cent. In all, 38 per cent of
dwellings were either unfit, lacked basic amenities such as an internal
w.c. or a fixed bath, or required repairs costing (at that time) £250 or
more. In comparison to U.K. standards, N.I. dwellings are grossly
lacking in basic amenities, and according to the 1975 Northern Ireland
Housing Survey, published by the N.I. Housing Executive in 1976,
17.2 per cent of N.I. households occupy dwellings with an insufficient
number of bedrooms — a burden borne mainly by manual workers with
larger families.

In regard to the latter problem, the situation cannot be relieved by
sending young children to nursery schools, because there are very few.
Northern Ireland has roughly one place for every seventy-five children
compared to one place for every thirteen children in England and
Wales.

A concomitant of all these hardships, and especially the housing
situation, is that the standard of health in Northern Ireland is lower
than in other U.K. regions, despite the fact that the Health Service, in
terms of staffing and provision, compares very favourably with other
parts of the U.K. The infant mortality rate, at 21 per 1,000 live births,
is 24 per cent higher than the U.K. figure (1974 figures) and these
overall statistics disguise alarming rates of infant mortality in specific
areas, particularly in the west. Omagh, for example, has recorded rates
of infant mortality of the order of 30–35 per 1,000 live births.

The purpose of pulling together these statistics is to emphasise that
if the troubles in Northern Ireland were to end this minute, the young
people of Northern Ireland would still be living in a society under
stress.

Perhaps the most popular and widely accepted accounts of stress on
Northern Ireland's children have been given by local psychiatrists, most
notably Fraser and Lyons. These authors have published a plethora of

studies (Fraser, 1971a, 1971b, 1972, 1974; Lyons, 1971a, 1971b, 1972a, 1972b, 1972c, 1973a, 1973b, 1973c, 1974a, 1974b, 1975) many of them frankly repetitive and methodologically limited. It must also be said, though, that these were widely received as valid comments on Northern Ireland as a whole, rather than as the more restricted, speculative exercises which they, in fact, were.

However, one cannot publish anything unless one has access to willing publishers and it appears that journals, for example, were queuing up to receive the latest offerings from these authors, to the extent that in 1973 the journals *Public Health* and *Community Health* published exactly the same article with exactly the same title by the same author (Lyons, 1971a, Lyons, 1971b), presumably to the same readership. Undoubtedly this keenness was due to the concentration of those authors on the more dramatic aspects of the situation as it was then, and the popularity of their work may have obscured more enduring and perhaps ultimately more important aspects of life in Northern Ireland.

At this point, therefore, much time will not be spent dwelling on the sorts of effects which Fraser and Lyons found as a consequence of children being exposed to rioting, shooting and bombing, since most readers will be familiar with the findings. In the main, both authors commented upon the general resilience of Northern Ireland's youngsters and the fact that the observed nightmares, enuresis and phobias appeared to be generally short-lived. This is consistent with the findings on disturbances among children as a result of air raids on Britain during the Second World War, where the stress of evacuation separation was found to be more disturbing than the effects of the raids themselves (Bodman, 1941; Burbury 1941; Mons, 1941, Bowlby, 1952). In many cases, the phobias were adaptive in the sense that they removed the children from anxiety-provoking situations and afforded them an opportunity to express their anxiety.

As one might expect, the evidence suggested that it was children who were already vulnerable who were most likely to suffer symptoms severe enough to require medical attention (Fraser, 1971a). This was also the gist of the findings with adults (Lyons, 1971b). In particular, having one or both parents themselves emotionally disturbed by the violence was a particularly potent precipitating factor. The particular type of symptom, according to Fraser (1971a), seemed related to the child's personality strengths and weaknesses; for example, shy and timid children might develop double vision, preventing them from going out on the street.

The main concern which these authors had was for the long-term effects on children of being conditioned to violence, having violence rewarded in troubled times by peers and, indeed, adults. As Lyons

(1973b) put it '. . . one might anticipate that when peace returns to
Northern Ireland there will be a continuing epidemic of violent and
anti-social behaviour amongst teenagers' (p. 167). This question will
be returned to later.

In contrast to the symptomatic approach, a number of analysts
have stood back from the vicissitudes of the present situation and
invoked amorphous, underlying currents in search of explanation,
although these vary in the culpability which they assign or impute to
relevant groups. Whyte (1978) has given a thoughtful critical analysis
of most of these theories. Milnor (1976), for example, has related
current difficulties to processes of social change. Spencer (1974) on the
other hand has put forward admittedly impressionistic evidence that
forces for conflict have arisen as a consequence of a somewhat retarded,
if not entirely stunted, process of urbanisation. Utilising classical
American sociological analyses of urbanisation, he argues, in brief,
that urbanisation, despite its social drawbacks, has aspects which, in
retrospect, would seem likely to be beneficial to Northern Ireland in
relieving current tensions. For example, urbanisation brings an increase
in the range of things considered secular as opposed to sacred, a more
rational outlook on affairs and increased social tolerance.

Spencer argues that both parts of Ireland are under-urbanised and
that Dublin and Belfast are the two largest villages in the western world.
He suggests that the strength of the communal conflict is related to
the strength of ruralism prevalent which the weak urbanisation process
has been unable to eradicate. Counter to urban norms, Ireland is a
country where the sacred abounds (although religion has been largely
secularised by symbiotic alliance with the political institutions), where
the rational approach to the profound problems of society is at best
regarded as naive and, at worst, sacriligious or treasonous, where myth
has a higher status than truth and where the sense of community is as
strong as it is in the countryside.

This informed speculation by Spencer is to some extent supported
by a study of 1,257 Protestant and Catholic adolescents, mainly from
Belfast and Londonderry but including some rural adolescents,
reported by Ungoed-Thomas (1972). This study used a critical incident
technique and sought to illuminate patterns of relationships and
behaviour among Northern Irish adolescents. Although much of the
body of the report is difficult to follow, the distribution of responses
by theme showed clearly that apart from the expected preoccupation
with violence, Northern Irish adolescents were unusually concerned
about social difficulties with strangers and preoccupied with their
families. This contrasts with the more typical preoccupation of British
adolescents with boy/girl relationships (McPhail, Ungoed-Thomas and
Chapman, 1972) and supports Spencer's contention that our modus

vivendi is more typically rural than urban. In this scenario, the resolution of the present conflict will, in the absence of other influences, be slow, incremental and, perhaps, inevitable as urbanisation advances.

A further group of studies have been concerned with the attitudes of Northern Irish young people to society and to each other. Cairns in a series of studies, has been directing his attention to the development of ethnic consciousness in Ulster school children, and he reports in this publication the course of his research into the development of ethnic name-cue awareness in Northern Ireland. Cairns and Duriez (1976) showed that ten- and eleven-year-old Protestant and Catholic primary school children, in a small town relatively unaffected by the troubles, were differentially retentive of information tape recorded to them by speakers of different accents. Catholic children had a tendency to 'switch off' at a standard English (R.P.) accent and Protestant children were similarly affected by a middle-class Dublin accent.

This study indicates that Northern Irish children are sensitive to quite subtle discriminatory cues related to their religion and national identity. And yet, as Jahoda and Harrison (1975) showed, despite these peculiarly Northern Irish propensities, there does not seem to be a generalised ethnocentrism as a comparison of Belfast and Edinburgh ten-year-olds' responses towards the concept 'Negro' revealed. In terms of the formation of attitudes, Cairns and Duriez's study gives a fascinating insight into the processes by which divergent cognitions can result despite identical cognitive inputs. More particularly, as the authors politely observed '. . . the result may have important implications for example, for teachers and politicians with RP accents when attempting to communicate to certain sections of the Northern Irish community'. (p. 442)

Jahoda and Harrison's (1975) study in which children from the Shankill-Falls area of Belfast were compared with a control group of Edinburgh children from a poor working-class area also used an indirect means of assessing attitudes. In this case, preference patterns to linear drawings dressed to represent various roles (e.g. soldier, priest) were elicited. The results showed a general Belfast antipathy towards the police, more marked among Catholic children, a distinctly unfavourable attitude towards soldiers among Belfast Catholic children and, in regard to the roles of Roman Catholic priest and Protestant minister, a strong antagonism towards the outgroup figure on the part of all the Belfast children.

Jahoda and Harrison's Belfast subjects were drawn from an area where, in recent years, violence has been a frequent occurrence. Their experience was demonstrated by the ability of Belfast children to recognise the bomb potential of such articles as letters, parcels and cigarette packets — a capacity almost totally lacking in the Edinburgh children. But what about children in the quieter areas of Northern Ireland, where trouble, if any, has been rare and limited? How do they perceive their environment?

A recent study by Cairns, Hunter and Herring (1978) compared five- to six-year-old children from a virtually trouble-free area of Northern Ireland with children outside the province, comparing open-ended responses to ambiguous picture stimuli e.g. a row of derelict houses. Compared to children from a South London suburb, the Northern Irish children made overwhelmingly more reference to terrorist bombs and explosions in explaining the pictures.

This study was small in terms of the number of subjects, but the results are suggestive and consistent with a study in Israel of children's attitudes towards Arabs in shelled and non-shelled areas (Ziv, Kruglanski and Shulman, 1974). In view of the large amount of time which children are estimated to spend watching television in Britain (Howe, 1977) and the violence-laden content of Northern Irish local news coverage (Blumler, 1971), Cairns, Hunter and Herring (1978) hypothesised that television was partially responsible for N.I. children's preoccupation with violent events.

This hypothesis was tested by comparing two groups of children exposed to Northern Irish television, one group living in an area of Scotland's west coast which can only receive Northern Irish television, with a control group from a Glasgow suburb where Northern Irish television would not normally be received. Five- to six-year-old children were asked to respond to the kind of pictures described above, and seven to eight-year-olds were asked to write an essay entitled 'Here is the news'. There were almost 200 children involved in the study and the results showed clearly the influence of Northern Irish television.

Younger Scottish children within Northern Ireland's television range made much more mention of bombs and explosions than their Glasgow counterparts. In the small Scottish island town where some lived and where televison may have been a particularly important source of entertainment, the younger children were every bit as aware as their Northern Irish counterparts of bombs and explosions, despite their literal insulation. The pattern was similar with older Scottish children's essays, the quintessential response being given by one young essayist with typical Caledonian brevity: 'a bomb has just gone of [sic] in Belfast and that is the end of the news'.

But within the context of Northern Irish affairs, there is really nothing surprising in attitudes towards violence and outgroups. A detailed interview study by Adelson (1971) of 450 adolescents from the United States, Germany and Britain, aged eleven to eighteen and of both sexes, showed that young adolescents generally have little ense of society, little ability to decentre and put themselves in the other man's shoes, even when the other man is a hypothetical person on hypothetical island. Younger adolescents in Adelson's study emerged s frequently authoritarian, even bloodthirsty, for example positing harsher and harsher punishments as solutions to law-breaking. Moral absolutism is the order of the day at this age. In some respects, the problem of Northern Irish society is not that there is anything peculiar about the attitudes of Northern Irish youngsters under the circumstances, but that such attitudes so frequently appear to persist into adulthood.

However, even this judgement may be too harsh. A study by Schmidt (1960) of school children in Britain, Israel, Germany and Switzerland provided evidence that historical political hatreds, even in the absence of current animosities, are the norm. Schmidt concluded that group loyalty itself 'is often responsible for irrational, unhealthy social animosity' (p. 257) and pinpointed the directing influences of the animosity as the home primarily, but also the media and the populist postures of political leaders. These ideas have a familiar ring, but it should be emphasised that Schmidt's studies were carried out in the 1950s totally without reference to the Irish situation.

Although Protestants and Catholics in Ulster do not constitute separate nations in any strict political sense, their separate education, versions of history, cultural activities, religious habits, residential patterns and political viewpoints provide sufficient basis to justify a comparison with cross-national studies, without implying any evaluation of two-nations theories (e.g. British and Irish Communist Organisation, 1971). And the fact is that other cross-cultural work has confirmed the general drift of Schmidt's argument that the development of such animosities and preferences is quite normal in children (Tajfel and Jahoda, 1966; Tajfel et al., 1970; Middleton, Tajfel and Johnson, 1970).

In some ways, the single most important question which has been raised about Northern Ireland is that of the effect of the troubles on Northern Irish youth, particularly those most closely involved in or exposed to communal forms of anti-social behaviour. At its most basic, the question is whether the experiences of the children and adolescents of Northern Ireland have left them resistant to the control of law or indeed any control, and whether they will thus create havoc in Ulster, even in the event of a political solution being found. Lyons (1973b) and Fraser (1973) have indicated on the basis of their early clinical contacts with children from strife-torn areas that this gloomy scenario is indeed likely to be enacted. From the quite different perspective of experience and research in Northern Irish training schools, Curran, Jardine and Harbison (Chapter 14) have come to much the same conclusion, expressing the fear that 'when peace and stability return, problems of anti-social behaviour among the young may emerge as a major feature of life'.

On the face of it, the evidence is that there are substantial grounds for such fears. The previously noted social conditions in Northern Ireland are almost all prominent among correlates of delinquency (West and Farrington, 1973). Jardine, Curran and Harbison (1978) note that official statistics show that the number of indictable offences known to the police rose from 15,000 in 1967 to almost 40,000 in 1976. There are, however, as these authors note, problems with the validity of official statistics on crime and delinquency as indicators of actual levels of crime and delinquency in a given society. But several investigations have yielded data on variables typically associated with delinquency and which may therefore provide alternative sources of information on likely current or potential levels of delinquency in Ulster.

All groups of delinquents have a poor record of school attendance (Wadesworth, 1975). A survey of truancy in the Belfast and North East Education and Library Board areas (*Report of the Interdepartmental Committee on Matters Relating to the Alienation of Young People*, 1974) found that rates of absence in Belfast increased by between 40 and 109 per cent during the years 1966 to 1974. This survey also found that unusually high rates of absenteeism were an urban phenomenon particularly associated with inner-city areas and working-class housing estates in Belfast. Caven and Harbison's (1978) recent survey confirms this, finding Belfast and Londonderry particularly high on absenteeism.

It would seem therefore that some areas of Northern Ireland, at least, have a truancy problem of serious proportions and, by implication, a delinquency problem. Boal (1974), in his study of the Belfast urban area, found that almost 18 per cent of children and young people brought before the court were under control orders in which educational problems were frequently cited. A recent study of one of the two male training schools in Northern Ireland by the Statistics and Economics Unit of the Department of Finance, Northern Ireland (Research Report, 1976) suggested that over 20 per cent of boys were committed for mainly educational offences.

Reading retardation and anti-social behaviour are also strongly correlated (Rutter, Tizard and Whitmore, 1970; Sturge, 1976). The *Areas of Special Social Need* study (1976) found, on testing all P7 (eleven-year-old) children in the Belfast urban area for reading retardation that 26 per cent were classified as retarded. This study also found that reading retardation was the highest correlate of the spatial distribution of juvenile delinquency, correlating at +.64.

Some studies have used psychometric techniques to assess the xtent of anti-social attitudes or characteristics in Northern Ireland hildren. Russell (1973), in a major survey of some 3,000 Ulster choolboys from throughout the province, found at that time that 50 to 60 per cent of primary schoolboys and 60 to 70 per cent of econdary schoolboys thought it acceptable to use violence for olitical ends. Fee (1976) examined teachers' ratings of over 5,000 Belfast children's behaviour using a questionnaire devised by Rutter Rutter, Tizard and Whitmore, 1970) and found Belfast children to be igh on 'anti-social behaviour'. Comparing these findings with similar tudies in London and the Isle of Wight (Rutter, Tizard and Whitmore, 970; Sturge, 1976), he found that while London children appear to xperience twice the rate of neurotic disturbance as do either Belfast r Isle of Wight children, on the measure of anti-social behaviour, the Belfast children were higher than the London children and considerably igher than the Isle of Wight sample.

Recent studies by the Northern Ireland Training Schools Research Group (Curran, Jardine and Harbison, Chapter 14; Jardine, Curran nd Harbison, 1978) have compared Northern Irish and other British ormal schoolboys and delinquent boys on various scales of the esness Inventory, an American instrument designed to classify delinquents and disturbed adolescents. The most valid comparison in hese studies is with the Scottish samples. The result showed that Northern Irish training schoolboys and normal schoolboys tend to have nore deviant measured characteristics than their Scottish ounterparts.

All of this evidence, taken together, appears to make a prima facie ase for the assumption of future problems of anti-social behaviour mong the youth of Northern Ireland. And yet, there are a number of problems in taking it at face value, both in the specific terms of the tudies cited and in relation to larger, more general issues in the Northern Irish situation.

First, as Jardine, Curran and Harbison (1978) note, the number of ndictable offences known to the police in Northern Ireland is still only two-thirds of the rate in England and Wales despite ten years of ocial disturbance and turmoil in Northern Ireland. If one looks at the igures presented by these authors for juveniles found guilty per housand of the juvenile population, then Northern Ireland's rate is imilarly two-thirds the rate of England and Wales for all offences, and only one-third for indictable offences, although there are differences n legislation which make indictable/non-indictable distinctions difficult for comparative purposes.

It is true that such statistics are generally unreliable and it is ssumed that Northern Irish statistics are somewhat more problematical han usual as valid indicators of real levels of crime and delinquency.

In regard to conviction statistics, this argument may have some force. However it is not unreasonable to argue that in relation to the official figures on the total number of offences known to the police, the Northern Irish statistics are likely to be reasonably accurate. One might assume that with the strenuous R.U.C. and British Army intelligence efforts in the province, relatively little is missed compared with other areas of the United Kingdom, although for the purposes of this discussion 'known' offences do not relate specifically or exclusively to juvenile offences. More generally, it does not seem reasonable to ignore hard evidence on the unverified assumption that one set of unspecifiable distorting factors is possibly more important than another set of unspecifiable distorting factors.

The link between reading retardation and juvenile delinquency in Northern Ireland found by the *Areas of Special Social Need* study (1976) also needs careful interpretation. The correlation of +.64 found here was between levels of reading retardation and levels of delinquency in a given area, not between levels of reading retardation and prevalence of delinquency in a given group of subjects. The correlation between the two variables in this study is therefore even more tenuous and incapable of causative or even directly predictive analysis than such levels of correlation usually are.

Similarly if one examines the comparisons between Scottish and Northern Irish groups of delinquent and normal boys made by the Northern Ireland Training Schools Research Group, one finds that of fifteen possible comparisons, eight show no significant differences; in one comparison Scottish boys appear to be more deviant than Northern Irish boys and of the remaining six differences in which Northern Irish boys appear more deviant, only three of these show a mean difference of more than one scale point. Given the acknowledged problems of comparability of samples from different studies and the fact that no details have yet been published of the Scottish sample, it would be unwise to jump to conclusions on the basis of this evidence alone.

More generally, however, there are problems with studies which look at cold statistics without a constant awareness of the political situation from which these statistics emerge. It is rather like putting the cart before the horse to look at aspects of deviance among the province's youth and to extrapolate from these predictions about the future shape of society in Northern Ireland. A more coherent and ecologically valid picture may emerge by setting such statistics firmly in the context of the circumstances from which they derive.

For example, the statistics on school absenteeism (Caven and Harbison, 1978) are more parsimoniously explained by reference to such variables as children's and parents' fears about the journey to school, children's fears about the safety of their parents in their absence, the involvement of children in conflict-related local problems and so forth. Indeed the statistics show that : (a) it is in the areas of greatest conflict, particularly Belfast and Londonderry, that absenteeism is at its worst; (b) children in the fifteen- to sixteen-year-old age group (in other words those most likely to be conscious of the dangers to their parents, their community and themselves during their absence from home) are most prone to absenteeism; (c) in the majority of unjustified absences (57 per cent), there was evidence of parental implication in encouraging the child to be absent and (d) almost half of unjustified absenteeism (45 per cent) is accounted for by girls, who are much less likely than boys to become involved in delinquent acts. This would not appear to be a typical, potentially delinquent truancy situation.

Again, those studies which have measured various characteristics of Northern Irish youth in the post-1969 period have made two implicit assumptions. First, that high levels of indices which are known to be correlated with anti-social behaviour in other societies have arisen as a result of experience during the troubles. Second, that these indices are predictive in the Northern Irish context of future anti-social behaviour.

The problem with the former of these assumptions is that there is no base-line data, no pre-1969 data against which to test the assumption. In other words, it may well be that had Northern Irish children been tested prior to the present troubles, they would also have appeared high on correlates of anti-social behaviour, such as Jesness Inventory scales. Certainly, one would be surprised, for example, if Belfast children had appeared any more 'soft' or less tough than their counterparts in Glasgow or London, troubles or no troubles. And the Jesness Inventory scales used in the Training Schools Research Group studies are, in some sense at least, measures of toughness in the colloquial sense.

This leads rather naturally to the latter assumption of these studies that these indices will predict future anti-social behaviour in Northern Ireland. It seems entirely reasonable to suppose that, given their known validity in other societies, they will also be predictive of anti-social behaviour in Northern Ireland. The more important question which appears to have been overlooked is how predictive they are in the Northern Irish context. The hard evidence shows that despite, for example, high levels of teacher-rated anti-social behaviour in Belfast school children and despite high scores on Jesness Inventory scales predictive of anti-social tendencies, the actual rates of delinquency in Northern Ireland are considerably below those in England and Wales.

Indeed, accepted correlates of crime and delinquency have never been very good predictors in Northern Ireland. For example, despite

some of the worst social conditions in the United Kingdom, or indeed,
Europe, Northern Ireland has been an area of relatively low levels of
crime and delinquency generally, and this is particularly evident when
one looks at serious crime. One of the most startling statistics about
Northern Ireland, particularly in retrospect, is that in 1965 there was
one murder in the entire year in the-province. At no time during the
1960s prior to 1969 did the total number of murders reach double
figures.

The most likely syndrome which accounts for this peculiarly
Northern Irish phenomenon is the strength of the churches' influence
and the fundamentalist religious values espoused by both Roman
Catholics and Protestants in Ulster (Rose, 1971). This syndrome entails
a degree of respect for, or at least compliance with, the authority of
elders uncommon in the British Isles. Some authors, for example,
Lyons (1973b) have simply asserted that respect for authority has
broken down completely, although this assertion remains unsubstantiated. Other observers, with noses rather closer to the ground, have
taken the opposing view that, in fact, mutual respect has increased as
young and old have become involved in the problems of their
community (Jenvey, 1972; Overy, 1972; Foley, 1973).

It is important, therefore, to look behind the facts predicting
future trends in Northern Ireland. For instance, despite the degree of
acceptance of political violence found in Northern Irish schoolboys
by Russell (1973), it was also found that 40 per cent of secondary
schoolboys and 33 per cent of primary schoolboys were already
thinking of leaving Northern Ireland when they were older. This
possibly indicates a degree of ambivalence towards the situation which
is not otherwise apparent in the survey. Research into the motivations
behind the behaviour of Northern Irish children, such as the study of
values by McKernan (Chapter 13) will contribute to a clearer and more
useful understanding of the future for Northern Irish youth.

Jardine, Curran and Harbison (1978) have made the point that as in
England and Wales, the vast majority of juvenile indictable offences
are 'crimes of dishonesty' and the political crimes constitute a relatively
small proportion of all offences. Indeed, taking this comparison a little
further, the correlation coefficient between the total number of
indictable offences known to the police in Northern Ireland and in
England and Wales between 1967 and 1976 turns out to be +.93,
indicating a surprisingly close relationship between trends in crime and
delinquency on both sides of the water during recent years.

Having said that, however, there is evidence of a need to distinguish
between politically motivated and other juvenile offenders. Elliott and
Lockhart (Chapter 10) show that despite the remarkably similar
socio-economic backgrounds of juvenile scheduled offenders and

'ordinary' juvenile delinquents, scheduled offenders are more intelligent, have higher educational attainments, show less evidence of early developmental problems and have fewer previous court appearances than juvenile delinquents.

It would therefore seem that fears of a consequent boom in anti-social behaviour among Northern Irish youth, even in the event of a political settlement, are largely unjustified. The sum total of the problem will be represented by the degree to which rates of crime and delinquency in Northern Ireland exceed corresponding rates elsewhere in the British Isles. The current evidence, when set in a context of traditional Ulster social patterns and the political situation in the province, would suggest that that excess may be considerably less than has been imagined.

Finally, it would serve research workers well to consider two points in regard to the stress which Northern Irish children face. First, as Taylor and Nelson (1978) have pointed out, there is a need at this point to consider changes over the time since 1969. When considering young people, it is not only circumstances which change with the years, but the entire subject population.

Second, changes over location must be taken into account. It is a matter of record that there are area variations in unemployment rates, emigration rates, levels of ill-health and housing standards. Equally, there have been marked differences by area of the level and frequency of violence to which young people have been exposed (Schellenberg, 1977). Furthermore, many commentators have indicated from experience that there are area variations in the strength and type of local out-group prejudice or feeling. That this is, in fact, so, was confirmed by a study of stereotypes in a sample of 1,680 subjects from Londonderry, Enniskillen and Belfast carried out by O'Donnell (1977). The sample, aged fifteen to fifty-five, was weighted towards the younger age-level and amongst other findings, there was evidence that Londonderry stereotypes are milder than Belfast stereotypes.

It is necessary therefore to avoid reifying the problems of the young people and to move on from the 1969 Belfast conception of Northern Irish society which probably is held by all too many international observers.

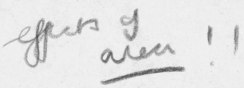

SECTION II
GENERAL DESCRIPTIVE STUDIES

3

Forced residential mobility in Belfast 1969–1972

Russell C. Murray and Frederick W. Boal

One of the features of any episode of sectarian conflict in Northern Ireland, particularly in Belfast, is the manner in which households in mixed areas (usually those families in the minority in the area) and those on the borders between segregated areas are subject to threats or direct attacks on their persons or property. The serious psychological effects of such pressures have been discussed by Fraser (1973) and Darby and Morris (1974). Many of the victims, however, escape the intimidation by moving elsewhere; accurate measures of the numbers involved are difficult to obtain but Darby and Morris (1974) have estimated that

the total enforced movements in the Belfast area between August 1969 and February 1973 is between 8,000 families (minimum) and approximately 15,000 families (maximum). Based on an average family size of four, the figure suggested by our investigation, this indicates a total of between 30,000 and 60,000 people who were forced to evacuate their homes — roughly between 6.6 per cent and 11.8 per cent of the population of the Belfast urban area.

A key, and as yet unresolved, issue is the efficacy of such flight behaviour in coping with the traumas induced by the intimidation. If it is successful then, other things being equal, there would be no reason to be more concerned with the long-term state of such households, or the children in them, after their move than that of any other group of households who have moved home. Intimidation, in its various forms, is undoubtedly harmful at the time it occurs and it can have significant social and spatial consequences (Murray et al., 1975; Boal et al., 1976; Murray and Osborne, 1977) but it may not have any long-term psychological effects once the threat is removed.

Studies of children exposed to natural disasters (e.g. Perry, 1956; Crawshaw, 1963) and early studies of reactions to rioting and explosions in Belfast (Lyons, 1971; Fraser, 1973) suggest that if the victims are able to take positive action to cope with the threat there is a much reduced incidence of psychological disturbance. It is the purpose of this paper, however, to show that even if the move is completely successful in ameliorating the pressures that occasioned it there are other grounds for concern. Moves made because of intimidation have outcomes which may differ in certain important respects from those made for normal reasons.

It should be made clear at this point that the data reported here were not intended to form the basis of a study of intimidation. They are taken from the findings of an extensive survey of the residential decision-making processes of Belfast households (Boal et al., 1976). For present purposes this paper has concentrated on those households with children who moved home between 1969 and 1972, and has contrasted those moving because of sectarian conflict with those moving for other reasons.

The sample

Of the 2,203 households successfully interviewed for the main survey 353 met the criteria of date of move and household composition. Reasons for moving were ascertained by an open-ended question. Two categories of answer were selected as bearing on the issue of intimidation. The first covered all answers which indicated that members of the household or their dwelling had been directly attacked or threatened with attack. This is the category referred to as 'Threats'; there were 72 households in this group. The second category, 'Troubles', was used for cases which claimed that they had moved because of the general level of conflict in their area but did not indicate that they had been threatened as individuals. In some ways, as will be seen later, the 37 households in this group, differ from those in the Threats category. Many of them, however, have come from a similar social and spatial milieu to the intimidation households and it is likely that it was only their timely departure that saved them from direct attack. In the results, therefore, these two groups were combined into a general 'Conflict' group. The remainder of the households, 244 in all, make up the 'Ordinary' group; these are the families whose reasons for moving, although very varied, did not appear to be related to the current conflict

The main survey employed a rather complex stratified sampling design incorporating a wide range of sampling fractions from 1 in 8 to 1 in 200. All the values discussed are based on weighted cases and not on raw cases.

Results

From the very large number of variables derived from the questionnaire survey those have been selected that might indicate potentially stressful factors. These cover three areas: the social and housing characteristics of the households, the spatial consequences of their moves and their feelings about their new home and neighbourhood.

Characteristics

This chapter is concerned only with households with children. It was found that those who had been forced to move tended to have larger families. For example while 10 per cent of the Ordinary households had four or more children, 35 per cent of those in the Conflict category had families of this size. The data also suggested that the Conflict households, particularly those directly threatened, may have contained a higher proportion of single-parent families. This referred to the situation at the time of the interview and not to the time of move. Thus it is not possible to say whether single-parent families are more susceptible to the pressures of intimidation or whether such pressures tend to accelerate the loss of spouse.

Conflict, and intimidation in particular, appeared to hit working-class households more heavily than middle-class. Almost 80 per cent of the Threats households came from social classes III (manual), IV or V compared to 63 per cent of ordinary households. Darby and Morris (1974) demonstrated that intimidation was most common in public housing estates and this is supported by further research (Boal et al., 1976). The typical household in such an area would be a working-class family with children.

Turning to the children involved in these moves the figures are consistent with this household pattern. Families forced to move through intimidation were more likely to have most of their children at primary and/or secondary school whereas the Ordinary households tended to have a higher proportion of younger children.

Perhaps the most significant information in this section was that obtained showing the type of housing in which the households were found after the move. The families in the Threats category were very much more likely to be in private rented housing (33 per cent as against 12 per cent of the Ordinary households). In Belfast terms this, in effect, means inner-city substandard housing.

Spatial consequences

In the analysis of people's moves Belfast was divided into a number of
sectors, each centred on a major arterial road, such as the Newtownards
Road, the Falls Road, the Shankill Road and so on (see map). This is
because research in Belfast and elsewhere has shown that a great deal
of people's activities take place within whichever of such sectors their

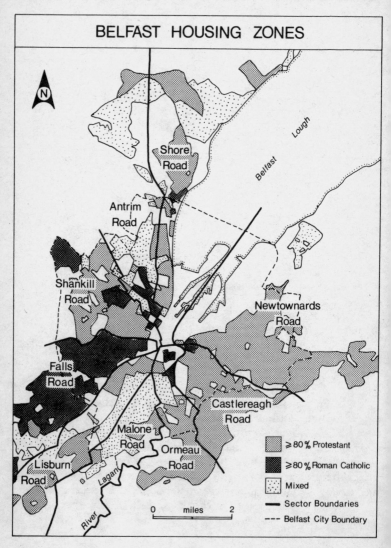

BELFAST HOUSING ZONES

≥ 80 % Protestant
≥ 80 % Roman Catholic
Mixed
Sector Boundaries
Belfast City Boundary

home is located. Their friends and relatives, their schools and recreational facilities follow a sectoral pattern and when they move to a new home they generally prefer to choose one in the same sector. This was true for the majority of the Ordinary movers in Belfast where two-thirds remained within the same sector. The Conflict families, however, were much more likely to move to a different, even non-adjacent sector and under a half remained within the same sector. Although there was no direct information concerning the effects of this on their social and other spatial links, except for the schools, it is very likely that for the Conflict families the change of house had a more disruptive effect on the web of their activities.

Information obtained relating to schools attended supported this. It indicated that forced movement was more likely to involve a change of school, particularly at the primary school level, than a more normal move. The effects of the conflict on school rolls through changes in neighbourhood composition have been commented on by Darby and Morris (1974) and McKeown (1978).

When the destinations of the different categories of mover were disaggregated by ethnic group to reflect the spatial realities, the information obtained demonstrated the preference of the forced movers of both communities for their respective ethnic 'heartlands'. In the case of Catholic households the sectoral preference was shared by the majority of all movers, whatever their reason.

Feelings about the new environment

There was no information on how the different children reacted to their new homes or neighbourhoods. Their mothers, however, were asked to rate the home and the neighbourhood on separate satisfaction scales. They were also asked if the neighbourhood had changed since they arrived and, if so, for better or worse. Levels of dissatisfaction found were higher amongst the forced movers, particularly the intimidated group who reported more than twice as much dissatisfaction as the Ordinary group of movers. This, and their perceptions of a deterioration in their neighbourhood, was a reflection of the type of area to which they moved and links in with the earlier material reported on housing tenure.

Discussion

In the absence of a specific study of intimidated households, and because of the small size of the sample, attention can only be drawn to certain features that give cause for concern; it is felt, however, that the conclusions accord well with the experience of other people who have been involved with the current situation in Belfast. It seems that even if, despite all that happened to them before their flight, the children of the intimidated families have suffered no long-term psychological disturbance (a highly optimistic and probably untenable assumption) the circumstances of the move and its aftermath may give rise to further problems.

Such children, when compared to their contemporaries whose families have moved for more conventional reasons, are more likely to have experienced disruption in their social and educational life. They are, perhaps, more likely to be in a single-parent family; they are certainly more likely to be in a low-income family. They are more likely to find themselves in a physically inferior and potentially stressful house and neighbourhood. The Catholic children in particular, although they are now probably reasonably safe from direct sectarian attack, are exposed to all the dangers of living in an urban battlefield.

One aspect of the problems of the forced movers that is not covered by this study, but which is well known to the housing authorities and social workers, is the high level of subsequent residential instability. Many households, particularly in Catholic areas where the demand for housing is greatest, have found it necessary to move from one temporary property to another. Another continuing problem is that of the impact of explosions on the residential areas. In 1973, for example, the Northern Ireland Housing Executive, the body responsible for emergency repairs and rehousing in both public and private sectors, reported that 14,000 dwellings in the Belfast area had been damaged by bombs in the previous year. In many cases the damage was such as to require the temporary or even permanent evacuation of the household.

Having pointed out some of the salient features of the subsequent experiences of intimidated families it must be emphasised that the problems which they now face, essentially those of a deprived environment, are not confined to such households. Most of the households experiencing such conditions today do so because they have been unable to find better acceptable housing elsewhere, not because they were forced to flee from such housing. Any policy to assist the intimidated families must form part of a general policy aimed at improving the lot of all families in sub-standard housing.

4

Responses to a behavioural questionnaire of a group of Belfast children

Frank Fee

In 1975 a survey of reading attainment was carried out on children in the area of the Belfast Education and Library Board who were in their last year of primary schooling. The opportunity was taken to gather other, readily available information about the children, and teachers were asked to complete the Rutter and Yule Scale B(2) (Rutter, 1967) with respect to each child. This paper deals with the responses to this Scale and relates them to the other information which was made available.

Emotional disturbance in Belfast children is obviously a subject of widespread interest and there is no shortage of comment about it, ranging from what one might reasonably regard as informed comment (e.g. Lyons, 1971; Fraser, 1974) to the wilder speculations of newspaper columnists. In fact no extensive study seems ever to have been carried out in Belfast into the emotional problems of children. There is, therefore, no baseline against which to judge the possible effects of the continuing civil unrest or other parameters.

Belfast, like most cities, has a complex social structure. It has 'deprived' inner city areas and more prosperous suburbs, but its social structure is made more complex by the presence of two communities with separate religious and educational traditions. There are, in fact, three distinct educational systems at the primary stage. The controlled schools, managed by the Belfast Education and Library Board, are all co-educational and, although they are open to children of all denominations, almost all the children attending them are Protestant. The Roman Catholic community is mainly served by what are termed 'maintained' schools which are not provided by the Education and Library Board but for whose general maintenance the Board is responsible. Those Roman Catholic schools which are not maintained by the Board are termed 'voluntary'. The teachers in maintained and voluntary schools are mostly Roman Catholic and almost all of them have been trained at Roman Catholic teacher training colleges. Fifteen of the fifty eight maintained and voluntary schools covered by this survey had principals who were members of religious orders. Only seven maintained and voluntary schools were co-educational. For the rest of this paper the term 'maintained' will be taken to cover both maintained and voluntary schools.

The third system comprises fourteen preparatory schools. These are fee paying and are usually associated with grammar schools. Only one of those taking part in the survey had mostly Roman Catholic pupils. Most preparatory schools have a significant proportion of pupils from outside the Belfast Board's area. Since the total number of children from these schools who could be classified as disturbed according to Rutter's (1967) criteria was so small (15 out of 289 B-scales) detailed consideration of the B-scale as used in these schools is omitted from the paper.

The survey

In the Spring of 1975 the principals of all Belfast primary schools and of eleven of the preparatory schools were asked to administer the NFER NS6 reading test to all their pupils who were due to transfer to secondary education in September 1975. Every principal co-operated and reading scores were obtained for 6,604 children. The principals were then asked to supply information about the sex and dates of birth of the children, their father's and mother's occupational level rated on the four point scale based on the Registrar General's classification as used by Rutter et al. (1970), the number of older and younger siblings they had and their attendance over at least one term. They were also asked to complete the Scale B(2) for each child. Not all schools were able or willing to provide the information or to complete the Scales, nevertheless information about father's occupational status was given for 4,632 children and the B(2) Scales were completed for 5,684 children. During the school year almost all the children in the age group, 7,301, sat the verbal reasoning tests which were part of the 11+ selection procedure. This procedure also included teacher's ranked estimates of suitability for secondary education scaled to the verbal reasoning scores for each school and converted to 'quotients' using the age allowance given in the conversion tables of the verbal reasoning tests. The verbal reasoning tests were themselves standardised over all the 11+ candidates in Northern Ireland to a mean of 100 and standard deviation of 15. As part of the 11+ procedure record cards for each of the children were forwarded to the Board offices. From these was gleaned information about addresses and the number of schools previously attended.

Results

Fathers' occupational status

The distributions of occupational status showed that for Belfast children generally a higher proportion of fathers was in the lowest occupational category and a lower proportion in the highest occupational category than in the Isle of Wight and in England. A higher percentage of fathers of maintained school children was in the lowest occupational category than of fathers of controlled school children (37 per cent as against 30 per cent).

Reading 11+ scores and other measures

The NFER NS6 reading test used in the survey was standardised over all the children examined. It was found that despite the lower overall socio-economic status of the maintained school children they did as well as controlled school children in reading and considerably better on the 11+ tests. The maintained children had a mean 11+ score of 99.9 compared to a mean score of 95.7 for the controlled children.

Maintained school children also appeared to be somewhat better attenders than controlled school children and boys were generally better attenders than girls. The difference in mean family size between the two kinds of school was very marked — families in maintained schools having an average family size of 5.4 compared to an average of 3.8 for controlled families.

Scale B(2) responses

All the completed questionnaires were analysed according to Rutter's (1967) classification into Antisocial, Neurotic and Mixed categories. The results of this analysis are set out in table 4.1 according to sex and to the type of school attended.

There are marked differences among the incidences of disturbance for the three types of school. The relatively low incidence of disturbance in the preparatory schools is not unexpected but the differences between controlled and maintained schools are surprising. The differences which are highly significant statistically are those between the boys from both types of school on the Antisocial rating and between the girls on the Neurotic rating. Many more controlled school-boys are classified as Antisocial and many more controlled schoolgirls are classified as Neurotic than their maintained school counterparts.

Table 4.1
Behavioural scale classifications by sex and type of school attended

	Antisocial			Neurotic			Mixed			Total			Pop.
	Boys	Girls	Total	Boys	Girls	Total	Boys	Girls	Total	Boys	Girls	Total	
Contr.	229	115	344	49	79	128	22	20	42	300	214	514	2703
%Contr.	16.9	8.5	12.7	3.6	5.9	4.7	1.6	1.5	1.6	22.1	15.9	19.0	
Maint.	122	99	221	39	32	71	18	12	30	179	143	322	2610
% Maint.	9.7	7.3	8.5	3.1	2.4	2.7	1.4	0.9	1.1	14.3	10.5	12.3	
Prep.	6	3	9	3	1	4	1	1	2	10	5	15	289
% Prep.	3.7	2.4	3.1	1.9	0.8	1.4	0.6	0.8	0.7	6.2	3.9	5.2	
Totals	357	217	574	91	112	203	41	33	74	489	362	851	5602
%	12.9	7.7	10.2	3.3	4.0	3.6	1.5	1.2	1.3	17.7	12.8	15.2	

Table 4.2
Behavioural disturbances — comparative results

	Boys				Girls				
	A–S %	Neu. %	Mixed %	Total %	A–S %	Neu. %	Mixed %	Total %	N
IOW	9.0	3.9	0.9	13.8	3.0	3.3	0.8	7.1	1279
ILBs	14.2	7.7	2.6	24.5	5.1	6.5	1.6	13.2	1689
Belfast Total	12.9	3.3	1.5	17.7	7.7	4.0	1.2	12.8	5602
Belfast Contr.	16.9	3.6	1.6	22.1	8.5	5.9	1.5	16.9	2703
Belfast Maint.	9.7	3.1	1.4	14.3	7.3	2.4	0.9	9.7	2610

Rutter et al. (1975) report a study using the B-scale on samples of ten-year-old children in ten London boroughs making comparisons with the previous Isle of Wight study (Rutter et al., 1970). Table 4.2 sets out the percentages of disturbed children found in both these studies together with the percentages for Belfast.

While the total percentage for Belfast is less than that for the Inner London boroughs it is notable that the total for Belfast controlled schools, 19 per cent, is almost identical with that for the London boroughs and that the percentage for controlled schoolgirls, 15.9, is higher than the percentage for London girls. Even with the maintained schoolgirls added the percentage, 12.8, is only slightly lower than that for London girls. It would appear that there is a considerably higher proportion of girls in the Antisocial category in Belfast than in either of the Rutter studies. This applies to both controlled school and maintained schoolgirls. There is a smaller proportion of Belfast boys in the Antisocial category than in the London boroughs although this is reversed in the case of the controlled schoolboys; 16.9 to 14.2 per cent. With the exception of the percentage for controlled schoolgirls, 5.9 per cent, which is close to the 6.5 per cent for the London girls, the percentages of children classified as Neurotic are much lower than the London percentages and in the case of all the Belfast boys and the maintained schoolgirls even lower than the Isle of Wight percentages. It must be remembered, of course, that the children examined in both the Rutter studies were one year younger than those in the present study and that it is consequently impossible to be sure of the validity of these comparisons. To this uncertainty must be added the earlier considerations about the differences between the controlled and maintained school children. It does, however seem to be reasonable to conclude that there is a real difference in the pattern of disturbance in Belfast in that where disturbance appears it is more likely to be of the Antisocial variety.

Scale B(2) responses and fathers' occupational status

The data indicate a clear relationship between the incidence of disturbance and social class with the lower occupational status children experiencing higher levels of disturbance. Similar trends were found when the occupational classifications were studied for controlled and maintained school separately. Table 4.3 gives the percentage incidence disturbance for each of the occupational classifications for controlled and maintained schools as well as the percentages of the overall population for each kind of school. Data relating to preparatory schools are not included since the small numbers of children involved and the restricted occupational range covered make percentages meaningless.

Table 4.3
Incidence of disturbances by sex and type of school attended

	Controlled			Maintained		
	Boys	*Girls*	*Pop.*	*Boys*	*Girls*	*Pop.*
N	248	177	2396	118	112	1921
I & II	1.2	.6	7.7	5.1	0.9	12.5
III	5.2	7.9	12.5	9.3	0.9	10.0
III	48.8	54.2	53.6	38.1	28.6	44.0
IV	44.8	37.3	26.2	47.5	69.6	33.5

The distributions of the two populations into the occupational classifications differ significantly, there being higher proportions of children from the maintained schools in the highest and in the lowest categories. The differences between the distributions of disturbance of the controlled and maintained schools may reflect this to some extent but this cannot be claimed to account for the preponderance of disturbed girls from maintained schools in the lowest occupational category. This is confirmed by the fact that the distribution of the disturbed boys from maintained schools is significantly different from that of their female counterparts whereas no such statistically significant difference is to be found between the distributions of controlled schoolboys and girls. Even the difference between the distributions for controlled school and maintained schoolboys does not quite reach the 1 per cent level of statistical significance and, if the difference in the population distributions of occupational status is allowed for, the difference is not, in fact, statistically significant. Here then is a finding which does not have a straightforward explanation on the basis of the data so far examined: disturbed girls in maintained schools are more likely to come from a poorer socioeconomic background than one would expect from consideration of the controlled school population and from the maintained schoolboys.

Scale B(2) response and 11+ success

The total number of disturbed children successful in the 11+ examination was 28 or 3.3 per cent of the total number of disturbed. The overall success rate was 19.4 per cent. Although a higher proportion of disturbed children from maintained schools than from controlled schools was successful the difference was not statistically significant.

Scale B(2) responses and reading failure

Table 4.4 sets out the percentages of disturbed children who scored less than 23 on the NFER NS6 test used in the survey. There was only one preparatory school pupil who was both disturbed and retarded in reading.

Table 4.4
Behavioural disturbance and reading failure

	Controlled			Maintained		
	Boys	*Girls*	*Pop.*	*Boys*	*Girls*	*Pop.*
N	131	54	2703	105	101	2610
Retarded readers	43.7	25.2	36.4	58.7	70.6	35.7

The differences between the respective proportions by sex for both types of school are statistically very significant. This is particularly true of the girls. It would appear that in maintained schools disturbance and poor reading performance are more likely to go together. This ties in with the finding that more disturbed children in maintained schools are in the lowest occupational category.

The discrepancy between the proportions for controlled school and maintained schoolgirls can be shown by further analysis to relate to aggressive disturbance rather than neurotic which is fairly uniform for both sexes and both types of school.

Correlation analysis

Another way of examining the relationship between the B Scale categories and the other measures is to consider the correlations between them. These correlations are presented in Table 4.5 for 20 per cent samples of boys and girls from controlled and maintained schools. Two additional measures are included, the first of which is simply the number of times a child changed school. The second additional measure included is the rating of each individual school depending on its situation in an 'area of need' as defined in the government document *Belfast: Areas of Special Social Need* (1976). Two levels of areas of need are defined: areas of special need and high risk areas, which generally border the areas of special need. One can therefore have three categories of school: schools in areas of need, schools in high risk areas and schools elsewhere. The Anti-Social and Mixed category is significantly associated with the responses to the Truancy item (No. 2) on the B Scale but only for controlled schoolboys and maintained schoolgirls is there a statistically significant correlation between this category and Father's Occupational Status. For both sexes and for both types of school the Anti-Social and Mixed category is associated with poor performance on the 11+ measures although this association is not particularly strong for maintained schoolboys. Its association with poor attendance is clear except in the case of controlled school boys. Only for maintained school girls is there a significant correlation between the Anti-Social and Mixed category and the BAN school ratings. The correlations between the Neurotic category and the other measures are generally low with the exception of poor attendance for boys at both types of school and truancy in the case of controlled schoolboys.

Table 4.5
Correlations between B-scale categories and other survey measures

| | Antisocial and mixed | | | | Neurotic | | | |
| | Controlled | | Maintained | | Controlled | | Maintained | |
	Boys	Girls	Boys	Girls	Boys	Girls	Boys	Girls
Reading	−03	−15	−19	−30	−09	−13	02	−10
11+ Total	−30	−20	−15	−34	−12	−17	00	−13
11+ VRQ	−30	−20	−12	−35	−15	−18	03	−12
11+ Teacher's est.	−32	−19	−17	−34	−11	−17	00	−12
% Attendance	−07	−27	−19	−23	−24	−14	−36	08
Truancy	32	41	48	28	22	10	−03	−02
Father's occ. status	23	14	−02	25	14	10	07	04
Family size	03	02	00	29	−04	−02	05	01
Mother working	07	−09	08	07	02	02	12	12
School changes	12	00	−02	−03	−04	06	−06	10
BAN rating	−02	−03	09	23	09	−04	00	05

Factor analysis

Using the method described by Fee (1973) the intercorrelations of nine of the measures were factor analysed to accord with a target matrix comprising a general factor and a factor of school attainment. The hypothesis behind the target matrix was the obvious one that much, but not all of the covariance of the reading and 11+ tests was associated negatively with those variables which reflected inadequacies in home background. The analysis was successful in the case of the maintained school correlations in that all elements in the postulated zero positions were in the range ±0.1. A third factor relating attainment and Father's Occupational Status was necessary in the case of the controlled school correlations to ensure a similarly 'clean' factor structure. The loadings of the two B-scale categories and the BAN school rating were estimated for the various factors. The factor loadings are set out in table 4.6. The first factor links academic failure with bad school attendance, truancy, large family size and, for controlled school children, frequency of change of school. This last is not significant for the maintained school children perhaps because these children changed schools very infrequently. It is worth noting that Mother Working is not negatively loaded on this factor. Academic level is much more highly loaded on this factor for maintained school children, particularly for maintained schoolgirls. This factor is also related to BAN rating for maintained school children but not for controlled school children. The B-scale variables are mostly loaded on this factor.

The second factor implies the interaction of school and child with respect to academic success independently of the other target variables and factors. The figures given in table 4.6 suggest that controlled schoolboys are least influenced by school itself and controlled school-girls most. On the maintained side BAN schools are slightly less successful than non-BAN schools particularly with respect to boys. Neurotic behaviour in girls is slightly negatively associated with this factor.

The third factor relates socio-economic status and academic performance independently of the other variables associated with low status and may be taken to reflect either inherited ability and/or negative attitudes towards academic success in the home. Why this factor does not apply to maintained school children is a matter for speculation. A possible reason is that environmental controls which affect attendance, truancy and discourage the production of over large families are less effective in the Catholic population.

Conclusions

Comparison with previous studies by Rutter and his colleagues (1970, 1975) suggests that overall levels of disturbance in the population studied, although much higher than in the Isle of Wight are lower than in Inner London. A notable feature of the Belfast results is the high incidence of Antisocial disturbance relative to Neurotic disturbance compared with the Rutter studies. There is also a great difference in the incidence of disturbance, particularly Antisocial disturbance in the case of boys, between controlled school and maintained school children in Belfast. No straightforward explanation for either of these findings can be derived from the data although had the study been confined to controlled schools it might have been concluded that the overall incidence of disturbance was similar to that in Inner London

Table 4.6

Factors from various survey measures (loadings less than ± .10 omitted)

	I				II				III	
	Controlled		Maintained		Controlled		Maintained		Controlled	
	Boys	Girls	Boys	Girls	Boys	Girls	Boys	Girls	Boys	Girls
Reading	46	24	74	79		69	55	34	73	39
11+ VRQ	47	37	76	87	20	74	59	43	83	49
11+ Teacher's est.	47	31	79	88	17	74	58	41	83	51
% Attendance	65	70	32	53						
Truancy	−54	−55	−21	−26						
Father's occ. status	−50	−26	−66	−68						
Family size	−35	−35	−19	−33					−36	−68
Mother working	16	19								
School changes	−28	−25								
A—S + Mixed	−22	−28	−15	−35					−24	
Neurotics	−18	−12				−11	11	−11		
BAN rating			−48	−41			−18	−10	−15	−14

but that there was some kind of effect, perhaps related to events in Northern Ireland over the last ten years, which, particularly with respect to boys, caused neurotic behaviour to be 'displaced' by anti-social behaviour in many cases. Against such a theory stands the results from the maintained schools and, perhaps the finding that there is, in fact, a lower incidence of Belfast children in the mixed category than in Inner London. Given the differences in how the Protestant and Roman Catholic populations are distributed in Belfast and the differences between the respective school systems differences in the incidence of disturbance might have been expected. Prior to this study however it was not predictable in what direction the differences should be. On the one hand, possibly because more middle-class Protestants live just outside the Belfast boundary the controlled school children examined in the survey seemed to be of lower average intelligence and for that reason a higher incidence of disturbance might have been predicted among them. On the other hand there were more maintained school children whose fathers were of the lowest occupational status and more Roman Catholic families live in the designated Belfast Areas of Need both of which facts might suggest that maintained school children should have shown the higher incidence of disturbance. The factor analysis indicates how these population differences may have been operating on the variables used in the survey. The loadings of the BAN rating for the maintained school children only on the first factor and the non-appearance of a third factor for these children may be a reflection of a greater degree of social 'streaming' with respect to area and school. This could be offered in support of the hypothesis, which seems sensible enough a priori, that disturbed behaviour is less likely to be reported in a school whose pupils are of a fairly homogeneous social background, even if poor, either because the incidence of such behaviour is genuinely low, perhaps because the staff of the school has learnt to cope better with potentially disturbed children, or because teachers have become less sensitive to aberrations of behaviour.

Considering simply the differences between the school systems with respect to single sex and mixed schools an hypothesis that children at single sex schools should show less disturbance than those at mixed schools would have received considerable support from the results of this survey. Had it been possible to eliminate the possible effects of differences in the populations such as have already been mentioned the extent of the support would have been less equivocal. Unfortunately in this context, all the controlled schools were mixed and practically all the maintained schools were single sex. The results of the factor analysis and other evidence presented suggest that the relationship between school systems and sex of pupil with respect to disturbance and, indeed, academic performance are too complex to allow a definite conclusion about the relative effects of single sex and mixed schools on the basis of this survey.

Although this study has been mainly concerned with two school systems which are the product of religious and cultural differences possible direct effects of these differences have not been discussed. It could, of course, be that the effects of these differences are important in determining the levels of disturbed behaviour or indeed of academic performance but since the two communities and their schools differ in other respects, until the effects of these differences have been fully understood it is clearly foolish to make general statements and difficult to make testable hypotheses about possible religious or cultural effects in Belfast primary schools. One must be sure that reported disturbed behaviour is not a function of whether a school is single sexed or mixed or of the homogeneity of the social class of its pupils. Some estimate of the relative sensitivity to disturbed behaviour of men and women teachers is also needed since in this survey probably no boys in maintained schools were rated on the B scale by women and very few, if any, girls by men whereas in the controlled schools both men and women were responsible for the ratings for both sexes.

The findings of this study can, therefore, be regarded at best as baseline data for further studies. It is, however, possibly of some slight comfort that at the end of the primary stage at least, the incidence of disturbed behaviour in Belfast, as far as the school system is concerned, high though it is, is probably no worse than might have been expected in similar urban areas in other parts of the United Kingdom.

5

Persistent school non-attendance.

Norman Caven and Jeremy J. M. Harbison*

Writers on the subject of school absenteeism have often bemoaned the paucity of detailed information on absentee rates. Such data as is readily available often does not differentiate between absences which are legitimate and those without legitimate reason but groups them together in one overall attendance rate. Such grouped data can also be misleading in other ways, for instance, in a school of 100 children a weekly absence rate of 20 per cent could mean anything from 20 children being off all week to all of the children being absent for one day each. Further difficulties are encountered in trying to assess the extent of what is sometimes termed 'hidden truancy' where a child may come to school, receive a registration mark, but leave long before the end of classes. Over and above this, of course, attention has been drawn to the numbers of children attending school in body but whose minds have long since truanted.

In spite of these qualifications, non-attendance at school remains one of the more important indicators of the behaviour of children and young people in society. It is an objective measure that is available (and relatively accessible) on all children within the compulsory school age range. There is considerable evidence that it reflects differences between schools (Carroll, 1977) and areas (Fogelman and Richardson, 1974). Non-attendance is clearly linked with educational performance (Fogelman, 1978) and other indices of anti-social or maladaptive behaviour at personal level (Tyerman, 1968) and in the wider community (Tennent, 1971).

Preliminary work (Graham, 1974) indicated that considerable change in school attending behaviour has taken place within Northern

*The authors acknowledge the co-operation of the Department of Education (Northern Ireland) and the Education and Library Boards in the preparation of this chapter. However the conclusions drawn and views expressed are the authors' alone.

Ireland during the present period of strife. A decision was therefore taken to seek a clearer picture of absenteeism in Northern Ireland schools, to assess the extent of the problem, to enable a valid baseline of behaviour to be established and to study the causes and implications of the problem and its relationship with other societal factors.

Figure 5.1
Northern Ireland Education and Library Boards

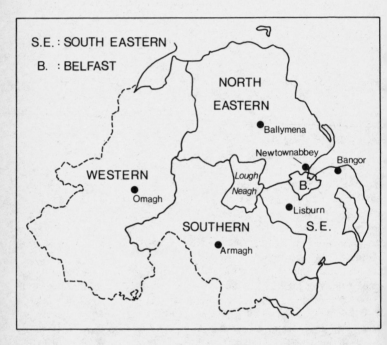

A survey of absentee rates in Northern Ireland schools during the Spring Term 1977 was conducted. Education Welfare Officers, in addition to their normal duties, recorded details on all children of compulsory school age who had missed more than 14 days attendance, i.e. three school weeks or more. In collaboration, where necessary, with the teacher most concerned, a decision was taken as to whether the majority of the child's absence was due to straightforward physical illness or not. In the case of those children whose absence was not in the main due to such physical illness the main reason for absence, taken from a pre-prepared checklist, was noted. This method entailed a number of arbitrary decisions: the selection of a single school term, the disregarding of 'hidden truancy', the utilisation of a 50 per cent cut off point for deciding whether absence was for physical reasons or otherwise and the introduction of a pre-prepared checklist of absence types. An additional limitation was that as most of the groundwork was conducted by Education Welfare Officers over and above their normal duties it was found impracticable to run reliability checks on inter-rater agreement as to the main reason for absence noted. The basis for such an approach was that it in part replicated Galloway's work in Sheffield (Galloway, 1976a, b) and thus provided a valuable means of comparing the significance of the Northern Ireland results.

The main results of the survey can be briefly summarised. The first column of Table 5.1 shows the total number of children, 26,556 in all, who were absent for more than fourteen days during the spring term.

Table 5.1

Absentees: age breakdown expressed as a percentage of the total school population in each age group

Age group	All absentees	Straightforward physical illness absentees	Other reason absentees
5–10	5.0%	3.2%	1.8%
11–14	8.4%	3.7%	4.8%
15–16	16.1%	4.5%	11.6%

This is broken down by three age groups — 5 to 10, 11 to 14 and 15 to 16 — and expressed as a percentage of the total Northern Ireland school population in that age group. The remaining two columns show the percentages for, on the one hand, those children half or more of whose total absence was for straightforward physical reasons — henceforth referred to as 'justified' absentees — and, on the other, those children the majority of whose absence was for other reasons, henceforth loosely, though perhaps somewhat inadequately, labelled 'unjustified' absentees. The term 'unjustified' absence is used in this paper for ease of reference. However the qualification illustrates two points. Firstly, included in this category are absence types such as school phobia and psychosomatic illness which imply that the children involved may require treatment of a psychological or medical nature. Also included are children who have a straightforward physical illness component included in their main absence type. Secondly, it recognises the view that 'unjustfied' absence is a label which can be construed as focussing the problem on the child, his family and environment and away from the educational regime, its values and methods, where the real problem may lie. Returning to Table 5.1 the major feature is the difference in absence rates for different age groups between 'justified' and 'unjustified' absentees. In the 5 to 10 age group 3.2 per cent of the total school population were 'justified' absentees as opposed to the 1.8 per cent who were 'unjustified' absentees. There was a marked reversal in the 15—16 age group: 4.5 per cent were 'justified' absentees as opposed to 11.6 per cent who were 'unjustified' absentees.

Length of absence was another variable that was looked at in some detail. Analysis showed that 19.6 per cent of the total 26,556 cases were absent for more than thirty days, i.e. approximately half of the school term. When 'justified' absentees were taken separately the figure dropped to 9.1 per cent of, in this instance, 12,300 plus cases whereas for 'unjustified' absentees it rose to 28.1 per cent of 14,223 cases.

Henceforth interest focussed on the 14,223 absentees assessed as being, in the main, absent for 'unjustified' reasons. Table 5.2 shows the breakdown of the group by reason for absence. The categories of

Table 5.2
Reason for absence

Absence type*	Percentage of 14,223 cases	Percentage of total school population
1. With parents' knowledge, consent and approval	57.3%	2.3%
2. Parents unable or unwilling to insist on return — parental knowledge but not consent	20.8%	0.8%
3. Without parents' knowledge and consent	12.0%	0.45%
4. 'School phobia'	1.9%	0.08%
5. Socio-medical reasons	1.8%	0.08%
6. Psychosomatic illness	1.4%	0.06%
7. Otherwise excluded or suspended from school	2.4%	0.1%
8. No answer	2.4%	0.1%

*Adapted from Galloway (1976a, b)

absence type are similar to those used in the Sheffield studies and it is noticeable that three absence types accounted for almost 90 per cent of all the children in the 'unjustified' category. Absence with parents' knowledge and consent, where there is evidence of parental implication in encouraging the child to be absent, accounted for 57 per cent of all 'unjustified' absences and represented 2.3 per cent of the total school population. Absence theoretically despite parental wishes to the contrary accounted for 21 per cent of 'unjustified' absentees but absence without parental knowledge or consent accounted for only 12 per cent of such absences and represented approximately 0.5 per cent of the total school population. This finding confirms previous research (Tyerman, 1968) that absence without parents knowledge and consent, in fact what some commentators refer to as truancy, is a relatively minor category of 'unjustified' absence from school. Other reasons for absence such as school phobia, socio-medical reasons, psychosomatic illness and exclusion whilst important in their own right are as expected relatively minor categories in the overall picture. It was also interesting to find that 45 per cent of these 14,223 children were girls — contrary perhaps to popular belief, fairly long absence for unjustified reasons is by no means an exclusively male phenomenon.

The data on 'unjustified' absentees was further disaggregated to assess the importance of geographical location — in this case a breakdown by individual Education and Library Boards. Analysis by geographical location indicates that in the 5 to 10 age group the Belfast Board absence rate is markedly higher than the others for absentees missing more than fourteen days but is not so accentuated for those missing more than 50 per cent of the term. In the other two age groups (11 to 14, 15 to 16) both the Belfast and Western Boards have the most severe problems and are joined in the older age group by the North Eastern Board. Rates of female absences over 50 per cent of the term are also high, for example 6.8 per cent as opposed to 7 per cent for males in Belfast for the older children. The Area Board data is by definition a grouped average. In the Western Board for instance with its mix of urban and rural schools further work has shown that Londonderry schools with their high rates were certainly instrumental in raising the overall Board rate.

The results of the Sheffield Study, which provided the methodological basis for this work (Galloway, 1976a, b), were compared with the Northern Ireland data. Table 5.3 shows the comparison between the unjustified absence rates of those children absent in total for more than half of the school term.

The Northern Ireland rates are similar to Sheffield in the 5 to 10 and 11 to 14 age groups but higher in the 15 to 16 age group. A more relevant comparison is perhaps that between Sheffield and the area covered by the Belfast Education and Library Board — both urban areas and similar in size of school population. The Belfast Board rates

Table 5.3

Children absent for more than half the school term for 'unjustified'
reasons. Comparison of the Northern Ireland and Sheffield studies.
(Figures are expressed as a percentage of the school roll in each age group)

Age group	Northern Ireland study Spring term 1977	Belfast education and library board study Spring term 1977	Sheffield study Autumn term 1974
5–10	0.22%	0.44%	0.26%
11–14	0.99%	2.16%	0.76%
15–16	4.63%	6.95%	2.8%
All children	1.08%	2.08%	0.94%

are considerably higher in the 5 to 10 age group and in the 11 to 14
and 15 to 16 age group are almost two and a half times as great.

All the results presented so far referred to both grammar and
secondary intermediate schools in Northern Ireland. The majority of
Northern Ireland schools have not as yet switched over to the
comprehensive system. The remainder of this chapter concentrates on
the secondary intermediate school sector where undoubtedly the
problem of absenteeism is greatest. A breakdown of absence rates for
secondary intermediate schools in the five Area Boards shows the full
seriousness of the problem within specific age groups in the secondary
intermediate school sector. Again the Belfast and Western Boards
stand out as having the highest rates, particularly so when the older
age group is studied. Absence rates of 11 per cent were found in both
Boards for the 15 to 16 age group of extreme non-attending children
i.e. those who missed more than half of the term.

The Sheffield study also attempted to identify some of the variables
associated with persistent absenteeism in schools. The proportion of
persistent absentees was correlated with the number of pupils on the
roll and the percentage of children receiving free school meals. The
Sheffield study found a non-significant association between persistent
absenteeism (absent more than 50 per cent of the term) and size of
school as measured by the number on the roll. In contrast socio-
economic hardship in the school's catchment area, as measured by the
percentage of children receiving free school meals, showed a high
correlation with persistent absence (r = .80).

A similar analysis was carried out for the Northern Ireland data. The
results show that there is no correlation between school size and
absence rates in Northern Ireland, confirming the Sheffield results.
Size of school therefore seems to have no direct bearing on absentee

ates. The high correlation found with the percentage of children receiving free school meals in Sheffield is not however borne out in the Northern Ireland data as a whole.

However, disaggregation of the data to Area Board level shows a more indeterminate picture. When this analysis is completed the absence rate for Belfast schools shows a higher, significantly positive association with free school meals, similar to the Sheffield results. The other Boards conform to the overall pattern of no correlation of absence rates with free school meals.

In addition, the availability of data on a number of socio-economic indicators derived from the census and other sources collected for use in the Belfast Areas of Special Social Need Study (1976) has facilitated comparison of these variables with the absentee data collected during the 1977 survey. This has permitted an assessment of the relationship between background economic and social factors and absence rates to be made.

Data on various socio-economic indicators was available on a ward basis covering the Belfast Urban Area (101 wards). The variables covered the areas of unemployment, housing, living conditions, education and personal handicap.

An initial problem in trying to compare these rates with the absentee rates for secondary intermediate schools in the Belfast Urban Area was the creation of a number of meaningful spatial units to which the ward data could be amalgamated as obviously not all wards had their own secondary school, and at the same time probably contributed pupils to more than one secondary school. The catchment wards of individual secondary schools were defined according to their feeding primary schools. The elimination of overlap by grouping schools together resulted in the final identification of seventeen school catchment areas or school zones for the Urban area. The socioeconomic indicator data was amalgamated to provide a catchment area rate for each variable and a correlation matrix was calculated.

The most noticeable aspect of Table 5.4 is that in few cases are there high correlations in the absent more than fourteen days category. In the over 50 per cent absentee rate analysis the situation is different, with numerous of the variables listed having high correlation coefficients, the unemployment and overcrowding variables especially so. Whether these differences in the degree of association between length of absence and background social and economic characteristics of the school catchment areas are indicative of two discrete populations is something which requires further investigation. In this case it is complicated in that children absent for more than 50 per cent of the term are a subset of those absent for more than fourteen days.

Obviously correlations exist between these variables themselves. The

Table 5.4
Correlation of absence with socio-economic variables

Socio-economic variables	Absence greater than 14 days	Absence greater than 50% of the term
Adult males unemployed	.54	.83
Juvenile males unemployed	.56	.84
Overcrowded households	.56	.81
Households lacking 1+ basic amenities	.59	.56
Owner-occupied households	−.43	−.67
No school examinations	.24	.40
Retarded readers	.63	.72
Social class IV and V	.62	.71
Total births	.53	.74
Bronchitis mortality	.57	.48
Households no car	.64	.69
Free school meals	.64	.87

Belfast Areas of Special Social Need report employed a wide range of social need variables and using a factor analytic technique identified four significant composite groups of closely related indicators. These factors were described as an unemployment-low family income factor, a substandard housing-poor physical environment factor, a personal handicap factor and an educational disadvantage factor. A social need variable representative of each factor was selected – juvenile male unemployment, households lacking one or more basic amenities, free school meals and retarded readers. These variables have been mapped on the seventeen school zones basis using a standard score technique which permits a comparison between the spatial distribution of each variable and the two indicators of absenteeism.

Figures 5.2 and 5.3 compare the spatial distribution of absence rates for secondary intermediate school zones in the Belfast Urban Area. All the zones above the mean in Figure 5.2 – children absent for more than 50 per cent of the term, are also above the mean in Figure 5.3 – children absent for more than fourteen days. The map detailing absence for more than 50 per cent of the school term shows a spatial concentration in the inner zones of the city's southern sector and in all the zones of the western sector.

This distribution can be compared with similar maps produced of selected variables from the Areas of Special Social Need Study referred to earlier. In Figure 5.4 juvenile male unemployment is mapped. It can be seen that four of the five zones with values above the mean for absence greater than 50 per cent of the term are also above the mean for juvenile male unemployment. Other indicators show similar patterns, for example households lacking one or more basic amenities, retarded

Figure 5.2

Children absent for more than 50 per cent of the spring term 1977

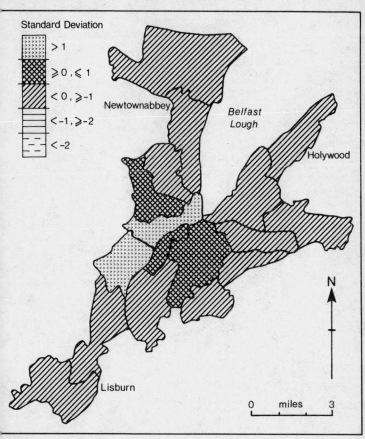

readers, and children in receipt of free school meals.

It is important to note that these results refer to measures of association, not statements of causation. In fact casual explanations of persistent absenteeism have developed along three inter-related strands — one which sees the problem as arising from the child himself, one which stresses the environmental and home milieu and another which sees the root of the problem in the school at both the particular (e.g. unsympathetic teacher) and general (e.g. school ethos, curriculum) level. For individual children any one or more of these theories may be applicable; the end result of absence from school may have various and interrelated causes.

Figure 5.3
Children absent for more than 14 days of the spring term 1977

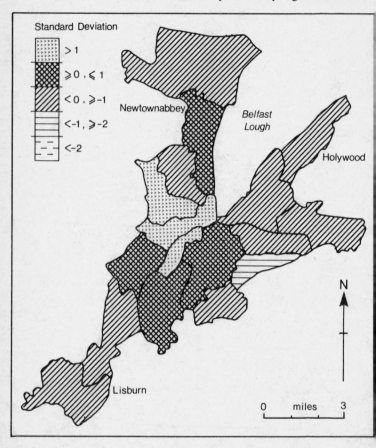

The role of this research has been to help focus the problem not to solve it. The first part of this paper presented a census and classification of persistent absentees recognising that the causal factors involved in each manifestation could be varied. The second part of the paper considered the relationship between various school, social and economic variables and absenteeism rates. School size was shown generally to have no positive relation with absence rates or free school meals (an hypothesised indicator of socio-economic hardship in the catchment area) when the Northern Ireland data as a whole was taken. However, in Belfast there was a correlation coefficient of r = .60 between free school meals and absence rates. This confirmed previous

Figure 5.4
Juvenile males unemployed

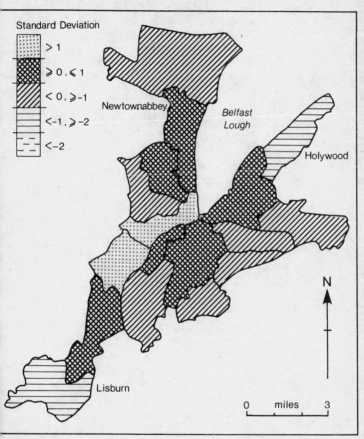

search in Sheffield. Other variables of a social and economic nature
ere considered in relation to absence rates for secondary intermediate
chools in the Belfast area. Correlation of these variables on a school
one basis with absence rates over 50 per cent gave high values with
nemployment, household conditions and low educational standards.
A number of indicator variables with acceptably low levels of inter-
orrelation were selected for mapping. Zones with values above the
nean for absence rates in excess of 50 per cent of the term showed a
igh degree of concordance with juvenile male unemployment, house-
olds lacking basic amenities, retarded readers and free school meals.
These findings lend substance to the idea that certain socio-economic

environmental factors are associated with areas with high absentee rates but leaves unresolved the question of causation.

In conclusion, research of this nature if perhaps useful in high-lighting and describing the problem and identifying areas for worthwhile future investigation. For instance, why is it that on yet further dissaggregation some schools are more successful than others in holding their children even though their catchment areas may be similar in terms of socio-economic composition? Other research must address the question of causation at the level of the individual. The present research is being extended to examine absentee problems at the individual school level and is following up a group of 'unjustified' non attenders identified in the 1977 survey, interviewing the child himself/herself, their parents, teachers and Education Welfare Officers. The progress of 1,200 children of primary school age identified in the 1977 survey as poor attenders is also being monitored.

6

Some aspects of occupational choice/placement of sixteen-year-old boys in Belfast

Willie Thompson, Bob Cormack and Bob Osborne*

The competition for jobs has been one of the relatively unexplored aspects of the conflict in Northern Ireland. For many years there has been a clearly articulated feeling in the Catholic community that Catholics are actively discriminated against by employers in both the public and private sectors and the evidence suggests that Catholic disadvantage in the labour market is a fact (Miller, 1978; Aunger, 1975).

After almost ten years of the 'Troubles' it seemed that some examination of the attitudes towards and experiences of that labour market was necessary. The findings reported here were obtained from part of a project set up to examine these aspects of the current employment situation. The occupational choice/placement of sixteen-year-old male school leavers was the focus of the study.

In their attempts to find regularities and patterns in the way in which individuals react to the job opportunities in society psychologists have used four main approaches. The decision theory approach views the individual as choosing, with various degrees of decision making skill, the vocational alternative that offers the greatest rewards (Gelatt, 1972). The trait and factor approach perceives the individual as moving towards a job which requires the 'traits' which he offers in his work personality (Lofquist and Dawis, 1969). In the needs approach the individual tries to satisfy his needs in a job. The type of need he will aim to satisfy will depend largely on his upbringing and family atmosphere (Roe, 1951). Finally in the developmental approach the occupational choice is seen as the outcome of the development of the individual over a relatively long period of time (Ginsberg, 1951; Super, 1957).

*The authors wish to acknowledge the support of the Fair Employment Agency in this research. However the views expressed are those of the authors alone.

These approaches are not necessarily mutually exclusive. While most psychologists would accept that decision making skills have a role to play in occupational choice, for some it plays a central role, for others it does not.

Sociologists have tended to look for patterns in the effects of the structure of society on people. These effects are conceptualised as being both attributes of individuals, as in the low educational and occupational aspirations of lower working-class children, and of society, in the need for educational qualifications. British sociologists such as Ashton and Field (1976) seem to be concerned with the working of the system as it is at the moment and how it tends to limit social mobility.

The psychological and sociological approaches may well be complementary. Individuals do make choices and decisions, but the limits to their freedom of action are to some extent determined by their differential experience of the social structure. Boys whose fathers are further down the scale of occupational status find it more difficult to rise above the limited and limiting situations in which they find themselves. The hurdles that working-class children have to overcome are much higher than those which confront their middle-class age mates, and their environment does not encourage them to build up the resources needed to successfully surmount the obstacles which society puts in their way.

However, both psychologists and sociologists have been slow to recognise fully the importance of the job market. This was perhaps understandable in the seller's market of the 1960s, but is clearly inappropriate in the economic climate of the present. Choice or placement are only relevant categories if and when there are choices to be made, or places to be found and filled. The market for jobs is now indisputably the central issue. However, economists have also been somewhat dilatory, especially in investigating the specific features of the youth labour market, and still seem devoted to the concept of 'economic man' who goes in search of pay and fringe benefits at the expense of all else. Unfortunately the real world is not so neatly packaged as academic disciplines and perspectives sometimes imply.

Adult unemployment is presently at horrendous levels; but it is perhaps less well realised that youth unemployment throughout the United Kingdom is an even more severe and less tractable problem. A government survey, *Young People and Work* (Manpower Service Commission, 1978) reports that:

Registered unemployment among 16- and 17-year-olds has risen 120 per cent between January 1972 and January 1977, compared with 45 per cent for the working population as a whole. Furthermore, the proportion of the total of unemployed 16- and 17-year-olds has risen as a proportion of the total unemployed from 5.4 per cent in January 1971 to 9 per cent in January 1977. . .

Youth unemployment is more intractable because this same government survey found that, in the event of an upturn in the economy, many employers stated that their first preference in recruiting new workers would be for experienced workers or housewives rather than school leavers. In an economic downturn many of the employers suggested that they would operate a 'last in, first out' principle — again to the disadvantage of young workers.

Statistics for Northern Ireland are given for 'school leavers' rather than for sixteen- and seventeen-year-olds but the two statistics are roughly comparable. Between January 1972 and January 1977 there was a 288 per cent increase in the number of 'school leavers' unemployed in the Province. In Britain there is at least some hope of improvement in the situation since the effects of the falling birth rate will mean fewer school leavers seeking jobs in the 1980s. However this demographic trend does not seem to be occurring at the same rate in the Province and thus the competition for jobs is likely to remain an important factor in the Northern Ireland situation.

This project selected to study the experiences of sixteen-year-old male school leavers in that competition and their attitudes towards it. Young males were chosen as the *Fair Employment Agency Report* (1978) indicated that Catholic males appear to be at a greater disadvantage in the employment market than Catholic females. It also appears true that the employment of men and boys is still a more sensitive issue than the employment of women and girls.

The sample of 350 boys included all sixteen-year-old school leavers in the four chosen schools. A response rate of about 80 per cent of the boys on the school rolls was achieved. It has not yet been possible to ascertain whether or not the missing 20 per cent form a distinct rather than a random group. However the attempts to follow up these boys would suggest that the group may contain a number of persistent truants. Moreover it appears that long term absentees are removed from the school rolls. It may be then that a significant group of boys may not have been included in the study.

The four schools, two Catholic and two Protestant, two in east Belfast and two in west Belfast, were matched as far as possible for size, sex and the social and economic characteristics of their respective catchment areas.

Data is being collected on the background context of the whole urban area and the catchment wards of the schools. This will provide information on the employment situation and other relevant characteristics which will enable a comparison of the structure of opportunity for the boys in the schools concerned. Pre-employment surveys were carried out in December 1977 and April 1978 in which data on the occupational status of the members of the boy's family, his occupational and educational aspirations and his willingness to travel to work in different parts of the city was gathered. This part of the study also included the collection of information on attitudes to school, work and aspects of society at large. Thirdly, a post-school survey was completed in October 1978 when the boys were interviewed in their own homes about their present state of employment. Their experiences in seeking work were also monitored and measures of attitude change administered.

This chapter reports the findings of the two pre-employment surveys which examined the boys' expectations of employment and their aspirations in that direction.

Results from the pre-employment surveys

The schools used in the study were designated PE for the east Belfast Protestant school; PW for the west Belfast Protestant school; CE for the east Belfast Catholic school and CW for the west Belfast Catholic school.

Employment status of fathers

In the two Protestant schools 74 per cent of fathers were employed as compared with 64 per cent in the two Catholic schools; however, the differences between east and west were even greater. In the two schools in the east of the city 76 per cent of fathers were employed as compared with 60 per cent of the fathers in the two schools in west Belfast. It would therefore seem that employment status of fathers is influenced by religion and area and that the opportunity for employment is improved by being Protestant and living in the east of the city.

While the current unemployment figures for Northern Ireland as a whole have now reached the horrific level of 13.5 per cent it is known that this overall figure masks the true nature of distribution of unemployment in the Province. Clearly, there are black spots where the experience of unemployment is at a much higher level than the provincial figure. It would seem that three of the schools are sited in catchment areas where such is the case. These pockets of devastating unemployment affect both Catholic and Protestant areas; but, in the present sample, Catholic unemployment is significantly worse.

In both religious groups more than 75 per cent of the unemployed fathers have been unemployed for more than six months. More than 90 per cent of fathers in employment in both communities have been so for more than six months. This would seem to suggest a high level of long-term unemployment. Such a pattern of unemployment is known to severely depress the sons' future employment prospects.

Father's occupational status

When the occupational class of those fathers in employment is examined, the pattern roughly follows that found by Aunger (1975) and the *FEA Report* (1978). There was a higher proportion of Protestants than Catholics in skilled occupations and a higher proportion of Catholics than Protestants in semi or unskilled jobs.

It is interesting to note that the east Belfast Catholic fathers have reached parity, as far as white collar jobs are concerned, with east Belfast Protestant fathers, but they have not made the breakthrough at the level of skilled manual jobs.

Job expectations and aspirations

The boys were asked what job they thought they would get when they left school and also what sort of job they might hope to get.

12 per cent in school PE and over one quarter in the other three schools did not respond to the first question. However when asked what jobs they hoped to get 94 per cent or more responded. This suggests perhaps that by the beginning of the last year in school quite a large minority of boys do not expect to get work when they leave school, though obtaining employment still seems to be an important aim (see section below on work ethic).

In a chi-square analysis of the expected occupational status of the boys the schools could be ranked PE, CE, PW and CW, while for occupational aspiration the ranking was CE, PE, PW, CW. In both rankings the first school was significantly higher than the last two schools. The Protestant boys in the east of the city have a more realistic expectation of employment than the others because of the location of employment in east Belfast, but the Catholic aspirations appear high in spite of the fact that they probably regard much of this employment market to be closed to them.

Perception of earnings

The size of the pay packet that a job commands is an important determinant of how attractive that job will be, and so the boys were asked to estimate the weekly income seven different jobs might provide. The jobs presented were labourer, factory worker, plumber, fitter, bricklayer, teacher and doctor. Analysis by 't' tests showed the Catholic perceived the rewards for each job, except that of fitter, significantly higher ($p < 0.05$) than Protestants. There was no significant difference between the two groups in their estimation of fitters' earnings.

When the estimates were further disaggregated by religion and fathers' occupational status there was a tendency for the estimates of Catholics and Protestants with unemployed fathers to converge (though all the differences which were significant for the whole population stayed significant). There was also a tendency for the estimates of Catholics and Protestants whose fathers were employed in skilled jobs to diverge. Protestant working-class boys seemed to be unaware of the high rewards attached to high-status jobs, Catholic working-class boys were not.

Work ethic

In response to the attitudinal questions relating to work and school the importance of work was demonstrated by both religious groups. More than 95 per cent in both thought a day at work was a day well spent; while 67 per cent of Catholics and 68 per cent of Protestants thought a day at school well spent. 90 per cent of Catholics said they would be unhappy to be unemployed if and when they could not find work, while 84 per cent Protestants professed they would feel unhappy in such circumstances. 60 per cent of Catholics (compared to 54 per cent of Protestants) indicated they would work even if they earned the same money as they would receive on the dole. The consistency of the responses to these questions between the two groups suggests support for the finding in Miller (1978) that attitudes to work among adults do not vary significantly between the two religious groups.

Discrimination

When asked if they thought there were any firms who would not start them because of their religion, 20 per cent of Catholics thought that this might be the case, compared to only 4 per cent of Protestants. It is interesting to compare this to the responses to a somewhat similar question reported in Miller (1978). Respondents were asked if they considered one of the main causes of the 'Troubles' to be the lack of job opportunities for Roman Catholics because Protestants are given preference. 78 per cent of Catholics agreed with the statement compared to only 17 per cent of Protestants.

Travel to work

Given the distribution of employment within the city the willingness to travel to work is crucial and thus the boys in the present sample were asked if they were prepared to work in any of five geographic areas of Belfast — central, north, east, west and south — and if the religious affiliation — Protestant, Catholic or mixed — of the area would effect their choice. Only limited definitions of these areas were provided and it was accepted that perceptions of west Belfast for example were likely to be different according to both the religion and the location of the individual. At this stage, prior to entering the labour market, east Belfast Protestant boys seem least willing to travel to work. These results, however, must be seen in the context of the location of employment in Belfast. The east Belfast Protestants have the largest industrial concentration in Northern Ireland on their door-steps and consequently may see little reason to travel. The east Belfast Catholics may see this industrial complex as closed, or partially closed to them, and therefore direct their attention and aspirations in other directions, notably the construction industry which would require travel.

When the correlations between travel scores, occupational expecta-tions and aspirations and school stream were examined, the occupational expectations of the west Belfast boys were significantly correlated with willingness to travel. For west Belfast Catholic boys the correlation between occupational aspirations and willingness to travel was significant but that for west Belfast Protestant boys just failed to reach significance at the 0.05 level.

Educational aspirations

50 per cent of the Protestants in the sample were not planning to enter for any public examination while only 15 per cent of the Catholics were in this category.

Discussion of findings

The occupational status of the fathers and its relationship with the expectations of occupational status of the boys presents quite a complicated picture. The two schools in the east have a much higher proportion of white collar workers (about 17 per cent) than those in the west (about 3½ per cent). The two Protestant schools have a much higher proportion of skilled workers among the fathers than the Catholic schools. The highest rates of unemployment are found among the west Belfast Catholic fathers, the lowest rates among the east Belfast Protestant fathers with west Belfast Protestants and east Belfast Catholics in the middle. These findings suggest that there are both area and religious differences being exhibited in the sample and support the decision to look at both variables.

The distribution of occupational status which the boys expect to attain is higher than that presently held by their fathers. Over 50 per cent expect to get skilled manual jobs though only just over 40 per cent of their fathers have jobs at this level. This expectation of access to skilled jobs at a higher rate than their fathers is especially noticeable in the Catholic schools where 48 per cent of the boys expect to get skilled work while only 32 per cent of their fathers are in such jobs.

It is interesting to note that while still at school only 20 per cent of Catholic boys thought discrimination in employment could affect them. If the labour market fails to fulfil their expectations, which seem high when compared to fathers' jobs, more of them may come to believe they and their co-religionists are the victims of discrimination.

The findings of the two pre-employment surveys suggest that the main area of competition between Protestant and Catholic may well be in the search for a skilled job. Just over 50 per cent of boys expect to get such jobs, slightly more aspire to them. It would seem that many boys in both communities will be disappointed given the present state of the labour market in Northern Ireland.

SECTION III
EDUCATIONAL PERSPECTIVES

7

Regional aspects of educational disadvantage

John A. Wilson

Educational disadvantage can be defined as the inability of certain groups of children to benefit fully from formal schooling. While children may be educationally disadvantaged for any of a number of reasons — forms of sensory handicap are among the most obvious — the condition has frequently been identified as a concomitant of social deprivation or poverty. As such, it has in latter years been increasingly regarded as a social phenomenon requiring a policy planning response. An example of such a response may be found in the Headstart programmes in the U.S.A., which had strong health and welfare as well as educational goals. Another example was the call by Plowden in the 1960s for a policy of positive discrimination in designated areas of educational priority. The more recent Belfast Areas of Need (Belfast Education and Library Board, 1978) programme, with its larger emphasis on urban renewal, is a further example of such policy implementation.

The present-day tendency to regard the inability of children to benefit as fully as they might from schooling as being closely linked with their out-of-school experiences or circumstances is by no means new. In the 1930s Burt's classic study, *The Backward Child* (Burt, 1937), emphasised the inefficiency of the mother as a key factor in educational backwardness. In 1945 Forbes drew attention to rural isolation and the prevalent Scottish dialect as possible contributory factors to retardation in language skills among school children in the Coleraine area of Northern Ireland. One hundred years before Forbes the Census Commissioners for Ireland (1843), reporting on the Census for the year 1841, had noted the demographic links between ignorance, or the inability to read and write, poor standards of accommodation, and the worst means of subsistence. The Commissioners for 1851 and 1861 (1855, 1863) confirmed a similar pattern of association, and the Commissioners for 1861, in drawing attention to considerable regional variation throughout the country in the percentage of persons unable to read and write, also observed that, as a general rule, where the population was scattered the schools were few, the distances between them great, the attendances irregular and the instruction desultory. In those years a state of ignorance was presumed to be due to lack of opportunity for formal schooling, particularly in the remote rural areas, as much as to the appalling social conditions of the time.

What, in the 1970s, are the hallmarks of educational disadvantage in Northern Ireland schools? Does the condition exist in an age of compulsory schooling from five to sixteen, and if so, what are its presenting features and circumstances? The present paper will examine this question at four stages of primary and secondary education. The evidence will be drawn from three investigations conducted by the Northern Ireland Council for Educational Research. Two of these investigations have been reported in full; the report of the third is currently in press.

In 1970 some 4,500 children in 115 primary schools were involved in a NICER research project in which school principals and class teachers, the inspectorate, medical officers of health, health visitors and educational welfare officers collaborated in making available or helping to gather the necessary evidence. The investigation was designed to indicate the extent to which home circumstances, parental attitudes, community or neighbourhood variables, and school organisation, teachers and teaching were differentially linked with above and below average educational performance as well as with general educational progress at two stages of primary education. The theoretical perspectives of the investigation and its methodology were shaped by the work of Wiseman (1967) and Peaker (1967) for the Plowden Committee in the 1960s. The main report of the investigation was published by NICER in 1971 as *Environment and Primary Education in Northern Ireland* (Wilson, 1971).

The report showed that Northern Ireland school children, at the lower and upper primary school stages, were both subject to and affected by the same kinds of environmental pressures as had been identified by the Plowden research. It was clear, for example, that educational progress was closely related to home circumstances, and that the educational ethos of the home carried particular weight. This does not mean that schools are unimportant. Rather, it suggests that primary school education has reached a stage of development where differences between homes are now much greater than differences between schools — hence the inordinate importance of the former. This represents a feat of differential social engineering. It also raises the serious question as to what extent the school can be used to redress the effects of social imbalances which are outside its control.

The evidence supported the conclusion that nowadays schools are more equally effective in providing suitable conditions for learning than are the pupils' homes. Nevertheless, it was found that for younger primary school children differences between schools were significantly related to a superior standard of performance in mathematics, and that, at the upper primary school stage, schools, independently of their social characteristics, differed significantly in their incidence of educational backwardness. Moreover, while there was close agreement between the two sources of evidence on educational standards, namely the results of objective tests and teachers' assessments, where the two sources differed it was evident that teachers might sometimes attach too much rather than too little importance to the adverse effects of a poor environment. For example, there was a strong indication that the potentially bright girl in a 'poor neighbourhood' school could be at a particular disadvantage because of a teacher's failure to recognise promise in unpromising circumstances. This particular chain of evidence illustrates the dual handicap of actual and ascribed disadvantage which can result when teachers uncritically equate slums with backwardness, and too easily assume that children from socially underprivileged homes are incapable of attaining other than a low standard of work.

The investigation confirmed that the able or potentially able child may be as vulnerable as the slow learner to the effects of adverse social conditions. Further analysis showed that, in a Northern Ireland context, unemployment and poor housing were key indicators of educational as well as social disadvantage (Wilson and Trew, 1975). It was also clear that, while children were most at risk educationally in urban areas of high unemployment and poor housing, the same kind of ecological relationship did not hold in the smaller rural primary school. This is not to say that educational disadvantage is non-existent in rural schools. It simply means that, in the less densely populated and socially more heterogeneous conditions of the small rural school, educational disadvantage is seen to relate more closely to the circumstances of particular families than to the circumstances of the school community as a whole. The practical corollary of this urban-rural difference is that, while a policy of positive discrimination may be practicable in urban areas of the province, in rural areas any such policy needs to be pupil-based rather than school-based.

Among seven-year-olds in 1970 a particular home variable which was strongly indicative of educational backwardness was the expressed preference on the part of one or other parent to have the child leave school at the first opportunity. This, in many instances, may have been as much a specific expression of parental disenchantment with the child's perceived lack of progress in school as a generalised rejection of the benefits of extended education. In any case, it anticipated at an early stage in the child's career the final gesture of the educationally disadvantaged, early leaving, which became the focus of another NICER investigation in the years 1972—4, when the school leaving age was raised from fifteen to sixteen.

That particular investigation, which was funded by the Social Science Research Council and reported by NICER as *Early Leaving in Northern Ireland* (Bill, Trew and Wilson, 1974) was conducted among some 3,500 fifteen-year-olds in fifty grammar and secondary (inter-mediate) schools in the province. It was conducted in order to identify the characteristics, cognitive and social, of those pupils who chose to leave school at fifteen but who, under RoSLA, would be constrained to remain in compulsory full-time education for a further year. In the event three groups of pupils, those staying on, those leaving, and those transferring to further education colleges for vocational courses, were identified. Following an investigation of the attitudes, backgrounds, abilities, attainments and school circumstances of these pupils in their final year of compulsory schooling the pupils were then followed up in the following year in order to determine to what extent they had acted upon their expressed intentions to leave, transfer or stay on. As it turned out, the vast majority of those intending to leave had done so though more, at 38 per cent of the age group, had left than those, at 29 per cent, who had expressed such an intention.

The leavers were largely from the secondary (intermediate) schools, and it was here that differences between leavers and stayers were most clear-cut. For example, the leavers had less favourable attitudes to school. They did less well on the ability and attainment tests. They looked forward to starting work and earning money in lower-level occupations than those to which the stayers aspired. Girl leavers in particular had a poor attendance record in their final year at school.

What, however, distinguished these two groups above everything else was whether or not they were intending to sit for a public examina-tion, whether or not they were regarded by their teachers as capable of doing well in an examination, and whether or not they felt they had the support of their parents for staying on.

Since that investigation took place the school leaving age has been raised to sixteen. Since there is every reason to suppose that the distinguishing characteristics of many of the sixteen-year-olds who left in 1978 are little different from those of the fifteen-year-olds who left in 1973, it can be inferred that those sixteen-year-olds who now leave school at the first opportunity will include among their numbers many of those who are least well equipped in the basic educational skills of literacy and numeracy. To that extent many of those young people are the end-product of a cycle of cumulative disadvantage, both educational and social, in an age of diminishing employment opportunities.

The investigation showed that the vast majority of leavers are now from the secondary (intermediate) schools. Indeed, as an unintended consequence of the prevalent bipartite system of secondary education in Northern Ireland, the most socially and educationally disadvantaged of our children are effectively segregated in the secondary (intermediate) school sector. This has been particularly apparent from the results of a recent NICER investigation which was concerned with how children adapt to secondary schools in their first year after transfer from primary school (Spelman, 1979). This adaptation process was examined for some 3,000 pupils in ten grammar schools, five area comprehensives, six junior high schools and ten secondary (intermediate) schools. The investigation took account of pupil attitudes to transfer, their perceptions of their new school environment, their social accord with their fellow pupils in work and recreational situations, and their educational and social standing in the school at the end of the first year.

In the area of pupil attitudes one study dimension in particular was found to encompass a range of apathetic or hostile evaluations of school and schooling. This attitude dimension, which was labelled *educational alienation,* was massively correlated with a number of school and home background variables, all of which confirmed a distinguishable gradient of advantage-disadvantage, social, educational and attitudinal, in direct correspondence with type of school, from grammar through comprehensive to secondary intermediate. Educational alienation was also in keeping with selection *within* schools to the extent that an identifiable anti-school sub-culture was characteristic of lower-stream pupils. This took the form of rejection by the group of those pupils who perceived themselves to be academically persevering, socially acceptable and good at games — self-perceptions which in higher-stream classes coincided with group acceptability.

A further feature of the investigation was its examination of the deliberate attempts by schools to facilitate pupil adaptation in three areas of endeavour: by developing strategies for primary and secondary school liaison; by instituting secondary school familiarisation programmes, and by promoting curriculum experimentation. Insofar as these programmes were most in evidence in the schools with the least-advantaged intakes, they represented a clear perception on the part of the schools as to where their difficulties lay.

This paper has attempted to illustrate, with particular reference to evidence taken directly from the Northern Ireland school system, how a pattern of social and educational handicap is clearly discernible from an early stage in formal schooling. The research has shown that the pattern has already taken shape even among seven-year-olds in the lower primary school. By age ten it is firmly established. The educational failure experienced by many children over the primary school years means that, when they transfer to secondary education, these youngsters are not only ill-prepared for transition, but are also thoroughly disenchanted with schools and schooling. They leave school at the first opportunity, feeling cheated by a system which has denied them a proper education. Their lack of educational and social skills is such that they are least equipped to survive in a contracting economic climate.

As has been suggested many, if not all, schools are aware of the problems and efforts which have already been made to do something positive to help these young people. Some initiatives may, of course, be more effective than others, and it is a responsibility of research to ensure that sufficiently rigorous evaluations of such initiatives are conducted as to indicate which are the more successful. For example, NICER has been attempting, in another project, still to be completed, to look in detail at the educational problems and difficulties being encountered and the work being done by teachers in a selected sample of primary school classrooms in socially disadvantaged areas of Belfast (Trew, 1977). The findings of this work should be of interest and assistance to the many teachers who are attempting to provide, in their classrooms, a more effective educational environment for the socially disadvantaged child.

There remains the question of what the schools can be expected to accomplish in the area of educational disadvantage. The available evidence would indicate, for example, that at the primary school stage at least, educational provision has levelled up to the extent that schooling per se has become a threshold variable, more detectable in its absence than in its presence when compared with out-of-school influences. Is one therefore to conclude with Jencks (1972) that since the long-term effects of schools appear to be relatively minor, one should think of school life as an end in itself and concentrate on making the quality rather than the outcome of that experience more equal? Many, of course, would argue that it is not possible to distinguish between quality and outcome in this way, given that educational outcomes are inevitably the product of a number of experiences in cumulative interaction. On the other hand, few will disagree with the thesis that there is a need to concentrate on creating educational environments that are adaptive to the needs of differing children, of whom the socially disadvantaged are, in this part of the U.K., a substantial minority.

8

Can we relieve the stress? A case study of intervention in an infant school in a troubled area of Belfast

Jean Whyte*

Since the early 1960s the interest in developing curricula to remediate deficiencies in the language competence of children from socially and economically disadvantaged backgrounds has resulted in a flow of reports on a great variety of projects from many countries. The evidence from a variety of sources seemed to suggest there was a need in Belfast for some form of compensatory education in language skills. It was decided to investigate the possibility of initiating a remedial language programme which could be used by individual teachers working alone in their own classrooms.

It was difficult to predict whether any of the forms of intervention already attempted would be effective in the Northern Ireland situation. Although most of the projects had as one of their primary objectives the enhancement of language development, and their findings were related to this objective, there were many differences between them. These differences were due to cultural and educational variables, to the backgrounds of the personnel, organisations and institutions involved, to the models of change adopted for the implementations of the projects and to the accountability factor.

In planning the project it was considered important to specify clearly the general principles which were to guide it. These were deduced from previously reported effective programmes such as those described by Cazden (1971). Close monitoring was regarded as essential so that strengths and weaknesses in the programme might be identified to provide guidelines for future action elsewhere in the Province.

Three general aims were specified for the project. Firstly, to

*The author acknowledges the co-operation of Dr Irene Turner, Department of Psychology, Queen's University, Belfast throughout this project.

establish whether a language programme could be developed on a small scale using resources which were already available. Secondly, to discover whether such a programme could be implemented by the class teacher and finally to assess the short- and long-term effectiveness of such a programme as measured by changes in the children and in the approach of the teacher and the school to language development.

A model for change

The importance of the teacher's belief in the value of innovation has not always been appreciated although some researchers have already emphasised this aspect of programmes for young disadvantaged children (Turner, 1977). In the present project it was felt that the key to success would lie with the teacher both in the short-term and in the long-term. It was necessary therefore to have a teacher who would welcome support and help in initiating changes and who would bring her own professional experience and skills to the project. The teacher's active participation in the discussion and planning as well as implementation of the programme was encouraged at all times.

Contact was made with a teacher who, with the support of her principal, was looking for assistance in developing a language programme for reception classes. Guidance in the structuring of the interaction was found through the 'problem-solver' model described by Havelock (1971). This model stresses the role and rights of the initiator, in this case the teacher, in a situation where changes are proposed.

Developing a programme

In the development of the programme, information was gathered on the resources and needs within the participating school, and on other language programmes which might be useful within the framework of these resources and needs.

Lack of financial assistance dictated the use of currently available resources, but this was likely to be the case in other schools where it was hoped the programme might eventually be used. Resources were classified for the purposes of the study as individual, material and organisational (in the school). The teacher was the principle individual resource and she had worked in this school for a number of years and had also taught in another school which drew its intake from a wider range of socio-economic backgrounds. Her attitude towards change was positive for she felt dissatisfied with the level of readiness shown by the children for the infant curriculum and while she felt that language was the key, she was uncertain in the promotion of extra development in that area, and was looking for ideas and support. She had participated previously in innovatory programmes for other areas of the curriculum.

While attitudes were important, it was necessary also to consider methods of teaching. Observations of current practice were made so that this could be incorporated where possible in the programme, as it was considered sensible to emphasise the value of the teacher's previous experience. Demands for a completely different approach or change of style might have created negative feelings and lack of confidence. It was hoped that innovations would arise from a growth of awareness in the teacher herself of possible inadequacies in present methods in attempting to attain new objectives which she herself had helped to formulate.

The third area in which the teacher contributed in the initial stages was in discussion of her current routine and her perception of her role in the classroom. From this and observation of the teacher at work it became clear that she was accustomed to working towards objectives which were clear to her. For this age group, the objectives were mainly in the area of social behaviour and in the development of perceptual and motor skills. She was also very active in organising and patterning activities throughout the morning in an atmosphere of calm. Finally she was continually involved in helping children to play and learn and in doing all the housekeeping jobs associated with this age group (4.0–4.5 years).

The second individual resource consisted of the participating psychologists who contributed their particular experiences and skills and made time available for discussion and collation of information from different sources so that planning could begin.

The materials available were those in common use in many infant classrooms — Lego, large blocks, construction materials, jigsaws and so on. They were adequately maintained and were produced for the children in a sequence which had been developed by the teacher. The classroom was large, bright and airy. Tables were grouped and different activity areas were defined. There was a large blackboard and a number of noticeboards in the room. The class had its own toilet facilities and storeroom and coats were hung just outside the classroom door. A television set was available in the hall.

These were noted because of concern that the programme should have an impact on the children through being based in the first instance on concrete objects and experiences which were meaningful to them and which were manifest in their own environment.

The school was a normal primary school built in the late 1960s

which catered for boys from 4.0–11.0. The principal has promoted
the notion of staff development very actively and also the introduction
of innovatory methods where he felt that they would be of benefit to
the children. Both children and staff were accustomed to the presence
of outsiders.

The principal offered full co-operation for the project, subject to
the teacher concerned being satisfied with the situation. There was
access to that teacher and her classroom at all times, and also to other
teachers and classes which became involved more briefly for pilot and
control purposes. In dealings with children and staff the normal
routine of the school had of course to be taken into account and
respected at all times. It was felt however that the study had some
advantages over some other reported projects, notably the Dundee
EPA project, in that detailed monitoring was possible by the researchers
and there was ongoing consultation with the teacher (Morrison et al.,
1974).

The school admitted a reception class in January of each year and
this was taken by the study teacher for two terms before the children
entered Primary I. There was no pre-selection, age and parental wish
being the only criteria for entry. The children had to have attained
their fourth birthday during the preceding five months. The usual
number admitted was 24. It was decided that the group entering school
in January 1975 would form the experimental group.

The effectiveness of the project depended on the extent to which
it met the needs of the children as perceived by the teachers, and the
needs of the teacher as perceived by herself. In the view of the teachers
in the school the children lacked labelling vocabulary and used
unorthodox grammar. They did not listen or respond adequately to
instructions and they did not remember what they were told. Other
studies have indicated that the main language deficit to have adverse
effects on the educability of pre-school children may be 'lack of
competence in grammatically elaborated and referentially precise
language' (Moore, 1972).

Although all the infant teachers in the school attached great
importance to language development, they acknowledged that their
choice of subject matter tended to be rather haphazard and that they
rarely managed to follow up children individually as most of the
interaction was in large-group situations. The project teacher felt that
she would like assistance in formulating meaningful objectives in the
area of language development which could be attained within a term.
A further area where she requested help was in deciding on content
which would cover important areas of knowledge, be interesting to the
children and encourage cognitive development if planned in a structured sequence. Finally, the teacher expressed her need for assistance

in finding means of implementing the programme so that every child would have an equal measure of exposure to it.

Although the approaches of different programmes designed to foster language in young disadvantaged children have differed nominally, there has been a gradual convergence towards a commonly acceptable core of content. This includes knowledge of such concepts as colour, size, location, shape and part-whole relationships as applied to concrete objects and events. It also includes the development of familiarity and ease in the use of language concerning these concepts and everyday objects and actions. The majority of disadvantaged children do not appear to have this knowledge at school entry.

A range of methods has been employed to convey this information to the children. There are two broad types of more focussed language intervention programmes, one in which the teacher's response is contingent on the child's response and the other in which the child's response is contingent upon that of the teacher. The latter more highly structured programme has been found on the whole to be more successful in teaching the crucial language skills. In such programmes the child, individually or in a small group, is required to interact with the teacher who is following a predetermined sequence of material.

Implementing the programme

Three aspects of language development were chosen for special emphasis. These were the ability to describe, the ability to narrate in sequence and the ability to explain some concepts and to use them. Interrelated with progress in these areas would be the satisfaction of needs in other areas such as that of achievement motivation, curiosity, and self-confidence, which would also help determine the methods used and perhaps even the materials adopted.

Evaluation procedures were agreed at the planning stage and were regarded as essential to support and guide the development of the programme. Three kinds of evaluation were envisaged and incorporated in the project. Firstly standardised tests were administered to the experimental group before and after the experimental period. These included the Wechsler Primary and Pre-School Inventory, the English Picture Vocabulary Test, the Draw a Man and the Boehm Test of Basic Concepts. Control groups were also tested. A second experimental group was taken by the teacher the following year, using the final version of the programme and these, like the original group and controls, have been re-tested annually. Secondly, a weekly evaluation was carried out on a random sample of the children to test them on the content of the previous week's programme. This provided information on the progress of individual children and also on whether parts of the programme might need repetition at a later date. The final mode of evaluation was the brief written notes provided by the teacher each week covering her impressions as she went through the programme. The findings were in all cases discussed with the teacher.

The programme consisted of ten units, each based on a theme. Each unit was to be administered over five sessions during a school week, one per day. Specific objectives related to vocabulary, concept development and use of language were listed for each unit. Ideas were provided for the teacher on, for example, the range of vocabulary which might be covered, on concepts which might be relevant for that particular theme, and on activities which might be employed during those sessions.

The class was divided into groups of five or six. Each group spent about fifteen minutes each day with the teacher covering the material specified in the programme. Different methods of grouping, of timing, of seating and of fitting in with other activities were tried.

After the first week modifications were made to the amount of material specified for the unit. Further reductions were made after the second week and the suggestions for implementation became, at the request of the teacher, very detailed and specific. She had found it difficult to work from an outline for a week and to ensure that each child had equal exposure to the same amount of material when her groups were so numerous and wide-ranging in ability and experience. The final version of the programme laid down objectives for each session, listed materials needed and suggested a line of dialogue which might be adopted by the teacher in teaching towards those objectives.

A reappraisal of the materials as the programme was being implemented led to the conclusion that in many cases they had not been designed with the present objectives in mind and so alternate materials were devised. Pictures to illustrate concepts were collected and questions written underneath to guide the teacher in using them to involve the children and hold their attention. Stories were written and illustrated to reinforce both vocabulary and the concepts which were introduced in different units. Ideas for using the stories were included in the text.

The finding with the most serious implications for programmes of this kind related to 'person power'. It is obvious that with children of this age a single adult can cope effectively, as indeed the teacher had been doing, if she is mainly organising the environment or teaching them together as a group. It was soon realised that it was an entirely different matter if one had a small group for intensive work while the rest of the class, some seventeen or eighteen lively youngsters, were pursuing other activities. It proved to be just too difficult for the teacher to give undivided attention to her small group in these circumstances. She needed to do so if she were to encourage their concentration and if she were distracted it made the tasks of selecting appropriate vocabulary, reinforcing each child, and motivating them all to participate actively, practically impossible. In practice she could not ignore what was going on around her and of course she was responsible for the whole class.

This was dealt with by the teacher consenting to the presence of another adult, in this case the researcher, in the classroom while the programme was being worked through. This person confined herself to housekeeping tasks and interacted with the children as little as possible in order not to bias results. It was felt that in normal circumstances, assistance in the classroom could be of tremendous value if adequate preparation, support and evaluation were provided, but since no assistance is available to most infant teachers, this was not explored any further.

Long-term effectiveness of the programme

Two groups of children have experienced the programme. Significant increases between pre- and post-test scores were found for both groups but particularly for the group who had experienced two 'runs' of the programme (the January 1975 entrants). This group have also maintained a lead over their controls, and the verbal scores obtained on the Wechsler Intelligence Scale for Children have consistently been higher than the performance scores in the post-experimental period. Their EPVT scores demonstrate more stability than those of any other group.

It must be remembered that the amount of intervention offered to these children — probably an average of an hour a week for ten or twenty weeks — was very little in the lives of these children. In the meantime they have changed teachers, some of them have changed classes, the style of interaction of the teachers has varied, and different aspects of the curriculum have been emphasised. Any indication of gain that has been maintained is therefore encouraging.

The teacher who implemented the programme and who contributed constructive comment where theory did not work out in practice worked from the notes which had been prepared in consultation with her during the experimental period. However she continued after its completion on her own initiative and with the support of her principal to put the principles of the programme into practice making further modifications in timing and content which had not been possible in the interests of consistency during the second experimental period. The principal subsequently was able to release her from normal classroom work so that she could devote her time to language development with small groups drawn from the lower infant classes.

Other changes in approach which were noted and appear to be enduring were an increased awareness of the importance of planning and structuring language work; an increased emphasis on language and language activities within the school; an appreciation of the value of using concrete objects and experience in stimulating the children's interest.

These encouraging results obtained from the implementation of a small scale language programme by one teacher would seem to suggest that the development of further programmes of this nature should be supported and carefully evaluated.

SECTION IV

ASPECTS OF ANTI-SOCIAL
BEHAVIOUR

9

Characteristics of a group of persistent non-attenders at school

Jeremy J. M. Harbison, Frank Fee and Norman Caven*

Persuasive evidence is available to document a significant association between school non-attendance and later delinquent behaviour; non-attending children must be accepted as seriously at risk as to the probability of their becoming involved in criminal activities. This evidence is reviewed by, for example, Tennent (1971). A number of possibilities exist regarding the relationship between non-attendance and delinquency: persistent absence may lead to delinquency as the child could have greater contact with peers already showing deviant behaviour patterns and the child has considerable time on his hands to kill, out of contact with socially approved activities; delinquency may lead to non-attendance at school as the child may be afraid of returning to school because of his offences; finally unjustified absenteeism and delinquency may both be symptoms of some deeper malady. A recent report from the Cambridge Study in Delinquency Development showed that truants, like delinquents, came from family backgrounds 'charac-terised by multiple adversities and have anti-social and deviant lifestyles after leaving school. It seems likely that adverse backgrounds produce anti-social people, and that truancy and delinquency are two symptoms of this anti-sociality' (Farrington, 1978).

Whatever the causal link, research indicates that an association exists. Work reported elsewhere in this volume (Chapter 5) shows that in certain areas of Northern Ireland school non-attendance is a major problem. Many children, notably in Belfast, appear 'at risk' on the basis of these figures. The present study was mounted therefore with two main objectives in view. First, to establish whether children subsequently identified as persistent non-attenders exhibited signs and

* The authors acknowledge the co-operation of the Department of Education (Northern Ireland) and the Education and Library Boards in the preparation of this chapter. However the conclusions drawn and views expressed are the authors' alone.

symptoms of this behaviour at an earlier stage of their school career (in primary school); second, if this was indeed the case, to study any characteristics of this group which differentiated them from a carefully matched comparison group.

The study

The survey of persistent non-attendance published in early 1978 (Harbison and Caven, 1978) identified approximately 4,000 young people within the compulsory school age range who were termed 'extreme non-attenders'. This group had missed at least 50 per cent of the Spring term 1977, the period of the study. Their teachers and educational welfare officers had rated the children as being absent for unjustified reasons, that is, straightforward physical illnesses accounted for less than half of their absence. The welfare officers and teachers further rated the young people on a number of categories describing the type of non-attendance. These included absence with parents' consent, absence without parents' consent but with their knowledge, absence without either parents' knowledge or consent, school phobias and a number of other categories. The survey indicated that non-attendance tended to be concentrated in a number of specific areas within the Province, mainly in the Belfast Education and Library Board and parts of the Western Board. The extent of non-attendance increased throughout the age range and was at a maximum in ages fifteen to sixteen. Whilst more boys than girls were unjustified non-attenders, 45 per cent of the total was female. The size of the study and resource limitations restricted data available on the young people identified to these broad characteristics.

In 1975 all children within the Belfast Education and Library Board who were in their last year of primary school education were tested by their teachers for the school psychological service. Some results of this project are reported in Chapter 4. It was clear, however, that this group of children aged between 10 years 6 months and 11 years 6 months in 1975 would have fallen within the group of children screened for persistent non-attendance in the Spring term 1977. It was thus possible to link the two studies and obtain considerable additional information on a group of young people identified as unjustified non-attenders. It was further possible, using this data, to examine whether early signs were evident in primary school which could predict the onset of persistent non-attendance over two years later.

In total 98 boys and girls were identified from both studies out of 125 children of appropriate age in Belfast selected through the non-attendance study (78 per cent). These were children aged between 10½

nd 11½ in 1975 and who were between 13 and 14 in 1977. Other
ork (to be reported) has indicated a strong association between
cation, socio-economic factors and non-attendance within the greater
elfast area. It was therefore necessary to select a matched control
roup, that is a group with the same proportion of boys and girls,
oming from the same sort of areas, schools and background as the
elected group of persistent non-attenders. This was done by selecting
rom the 1975 records of the Belfast Education and Library Board the
ext child of the same sex from the same class as an identified boy or
irl from the 1975 data. The comparison group therefore also com-
rised 98 boys and girls. 26 of the children came from controlled
Board) schools and 72 from maintained schools. (In Northern Ireland
rant-aided schools fall into two main categories, controlled schools
nd maintained schools. Controlled schools are under the management
f Education and Library Boards and the pupils are predominantly
rotestant. Maintained schools are managed by statutory committees;
Roman Catholic children for most part attend maintained schools.)
ecause of the way the control children were selected a similar
roportion exists in this group. This difference between children from
ontrolled and maintained schools is highly significant statistically.
ndeed, according to the results of the 1975 survey one might have
xpected fewer children from maintained schools to appear than from
ontrolled schools. (In that study a single rating of truancy was made
y teachers of every pupil and it was found that 9 per cent of the
hildren from controlled schools were rated as truants compared with
 per cent from maintained schools.) There were 50 boys and 48 girls
n the sample. This was not a significant difference but was in the
irection found from the analysis of the total province in 1978.

The following information was available on the group of persistent
on-attenders, the matched comparison group and for all children
vithin the Belfast Board. Firstly, a number of measures of intellectual
erformance and attainment. These were:

(i) an intelligence measure — the scores of the second verbal
     reasoning test taken at the selection procedure;
(ii) the teachers estimate of intelligence — at the selection procedure
     teachers estimate the child's ability and this is utilized along with
     the objective test. This information was studied as there was the
     suggestion that teachers might perceive truanting children as
     lower in ability than in fact they actually were;
(iii) the reading attainment scores at age eleven and at age nine
     (information collected in 1973);
(iv) the improvement in reading between ages 9 and 11 based on
     scores for individual children.

Secondly, data was also available on social factors. This information included:

  (v) family size;
 (vi) fathers occupational status (rated on a seven point scale);
(vii) percentage of fathers in the lowest occupational categories (Social Classes IV and V);
(viii) percentage of mothers known to be working.

Finally a number of measures of behaviour was available for the children at age eleven. These were:

 (ix) percentage of children classified by their teachers as anti-social and neurotic, as assessed by a scale developed by Rutter (1967);
 (x) estimates of truancy, trivial absence, and truancy or trivial absence, rated by the teachers on the above scale in 1975;
(xi) attendance of children, as a percentage of possible attendance, during final year at primary school.

(Because not all children had all information available, comparisons reported below are based on slightly differing totals. Levels of significance quoted are **P < .01, *P < .05)

Results

The first set of comparisons was completed between the selected control group and the information available (Fee, 1977) on the population of Belfast eleven-year-olds. An analysis of information on intellectual, social and behavioural measures showed that the comparison group obtained significantly lower scores on the ability measures than did the total population. The selected children also came from lower socio-economic households and had a poorer attendance record at primary school. This information emphasises the necessity of matching identified experimental groups of children from disadvantaged areas with appropriate comparison children.

When the control group was compared with the children identified as unjustified persistent non-attenders, a clear pattern of differences appeared between the two groups. (Table 9.1)

Whilst no significant social differences existed, the children later identified as persistent non-attenders obtained significantly lower intellectual and attainment scores and were rated as behaviourally more deviant than the controls. It should be noted that significant differences were shown by the experimental group even when tested (for reading) at age nine.

The evidence to date indicates that children later detected as non-

Table 9.1

Ability and behavioural measures for persistent non-attenders and comparison groups

Variables		Persistent non-attenders	Comparison group	Significance level	Variables		Persistent non-attenders	Comparison group	Significance level
Verbal reasoning score	M	86.1	92.5	**	Anti-social rating		25.2%	8.8%	**
	(SD)	(13.2)	(15.3)						
Teacher's estimate of intelligence	M	85.6	92.2	**	Teacher's estimate of truanting		40.2%	9.8%	**
	(SD)	(13.5)	(15.3)						
Reading attainment at age 9 years	M	88.9	93.5	**	Percentage attendance	M	75.24	87.88	**
	(SD)	(8.6)	(12.5)			(SD)	(19.2)	(11.7)	
Reading attainment at age 11 years	M	88.8	97.0	**	Teacher's estimate of truanting or trivial absence		65.5%	27.4%	**
	(SD)	(13.6)	(16.2)						
Reading improvement ages 9–11 years	M	−0.428	2.6	ns	Neurotic rating		12.6%	3.2%	*
	(SD)	(11.7)	(13.3)						

attenders were showing a number of signs of this problem at least two years earlier, at primary school. They were of lower ability intellectually, teachers perceived them as less able and they had inferior attainments at ages nine and eleven. Teachers rated this group as already absenting themselves much more frequently than their peers and significantly more of the non-attending children were being rated by their teachers as neurotic and anti-social. Equally important, however, no major social differences were found between the group — that is, they came from similar (disadvantaged) backgrounds.

Further analyses examined differences between male and female non-attenders at age eleven. The two sexes showed rather different patterns of characteristics; the boys were consistently worse on the intellectual and attainment measures than their comparison group. This was not as obvious with the girls, only one measure (reading age at eleven) differentiating the two groups. Similarly on behavioural measures the non-attending boys were rated much more neurotic than their controls. This was not the case with the girls. A comparison of th non-attending boys and girls showed that the girls' mothers tended more frequently to be working.

It is suggested therefore that sex differences may be important in understanding (and subsequently reducing) non-attendance behaviour. Boys appear generally more deviant in both ability and behaviour, whilst social factors such as having a working mother (and presumably being required for domestic duties) appear as important factors with girls.

Finally, some comparisons were made of the two school systems. A noted earlier the state system in Northern Ireland runs controlled schools, the voluntary system maintained schools. These predominantly cater for Protestant and Roman Catholic children respectively.

The selected sample, as already noted, contained significantly more maintained children than expected by chance. Analysis of the control group showed, as expected, that the children from the 'maintained' schools cam from larger families, had father's in lower occupational positions and had fewer mothers working than did children from controlled schools.

When a similar comparison was made of the experimental group of non-attenders a number of interesting differences appeared. While the social and behavioural indicators did not distinguish between the two groups, on all the indicators of intellectual ability and attainment the maintained children faired less well. The differences were significant on the two measures of reading age. The implications of this are discussed below.

Conclusions

In regard to the objectives of the study, a number of conclusions can be reached. The contrast between the children selected as a comparison group and all Belfast children tested at age eleven is interesting. It confirms the necessity of having a matched control group in that the analyses show that the comparison children themselves had lower academic levels than the total population, they came from lower socio-economic backgrounds and had worse attendance levels than that of all Belfast eleven-year-olds.

The group of persistent absentees identified was 'worse' than the comparison group on all the variables measured. The absentees were lower on intellectual functioning and reading levels, including reading levels measured over four years before they were identified as persistent non-attenders. On all the various measures of behaviour used, the non-attending group was significantly worse than the comparison group. It would therefore appear that children identified as extreme persistent non-attenders at age thirteen to fourteen were exhibiting abnormal behaviour patterns at least two years earlier. For example, on a very simple teacher rating scale two-thirds of this group was identified as 'at risk' in 1975 for truancy compared to only a quarter of the comparison group. The social measures available showed little difference between the two groups.

The present study also suggests that persistent non-attendance may require to be understood rather differently for boys than for girls. The fact of having a working mother was significant with girls and it may be the case that there is some pressure on girls not to attend school when other children have to be minded and the mother is not available. Boys and girls also differ on a number of other factors. Boys are more retarded intellectually and in terms of school performance than are girls, and the evidence suggests that individual behavioural abnormalities are more significant for boys than girls. There is thus some evidence that later persistent non-attendance by girls may be more related to environmental and home pressures whilst individual maladjustment, in terms of social, emotional and educational development, is of greater importance for boys.

An analysis of the type of school that the children attended showed that, for the comparison group the parents of the children from maintained schools came from lower socio-economic levels than did the parents of the controlled school children. Average family size was considerably greater for the maintained children's families and less maintained families had mothers who were known to be working than did the controlled childrens' parents. When similar analyses were completed for children identified as non-attenders, a different pattern emerged. The children from maintained schools showed consistently poorer academic performance than did the controlled children, though the results only reached significance for reading ages at nine and eleven. Equally, preciously found social differences did not apply for this group. Differences were not found between average family size, between socio-economic level of families nor between percentages of mothers working. The differences which did exist, however, were in the expected direction. An interesting but possibly less obvious conclusion to be drawn from the results is that, despite the fact that overall attendance levels were similar for maintained and controlled primary schools in 1975, significantly more maintained school children become persistent absentees. The information suggests that whilst this is not obvious at age eleven the behaviour is already established and develops rapidly during the first two years of secondary school. This information may relate to recent studies emphasising the importance of the school itself — for example Carroll (1977). In these the emphasis is on understanding factors operating within individual schools which may contain, exacerbate or possibly even generate persistent non-attending behaviour. The results may also represent some aspects of the differential situation existing for the different communities in Belfast. At the time of the survey the social controls existing for children from maintained and 'controlled' systems were different. Educational welfare officers, for example, were much more active within the controlled catchment areas. Thus the fact that this study found the maintained children lower in attainments may indicate that when controls break down those most at risk are the duller children. A further speculation is that if the curriculum is not meaningful, this is of greatest impact for the less bright children and, again, places them at risk in the community.

In conclusion, the present study confirms previous work by indicating that not only do children who are identified as unjustified non-attenders come from disadvantaged socio-economic backgrounds, but that even when these factors are controlled the non-attenders are still significantly different from other children with similar background. Even at relatively early stages in their educational career they are less able intellectually and have made less progress in terms of educational attainments. They also exhibit behavioural problems in their final year at primary school of such a nature and extent that they can be identified with considerable accuracy by their teachers. Their level of attendance is already unsatisfactory, for example, the average attendance of all eleven-year-olds was over 91 per cent, it was 87 per cent for the comparison group coming from the similar socio-economic background as the non-attenders, and only 72 per cent for the group later identified as extreme problem children. Both sex and school

ferences appear important in affecting the nature and type of non-
tendance and in any more detailed study of the link between
n-attendance and the development of delinquent behaviour these
e factors which must be examined.

For the community, the results would suggest that not only is the
k between delinquency and truancy complex, but that a number of
ctors must be involved in the generation of persistent non-attendance
personal characteristics of the child, social factors of the family and
ighbourhood, school linked variables and finally the wider cultural-
cial environment. It also highlights the need for early and accurate
entification and intervention in the problems.

10

Characteristics of scheduled offenders and juvenile delinquents

Ruth Elliott and William H. Lockhart*

The Emergency Provisions Act was introduced into Northern Ireland in 1973. In a sense this identified a new type of offender in that most of the offences listed in it could be carried out for political means. It was by coincidence that in the same year the first assessment centre for juvenile offenders was opened and it was inevitable some offenders whose offences were covered by the Emergency Provisions Act were admitted to the unit.

The present study compares the personal and family characteristics of a group of forty-two young scheduled offenders with a control group of delinquent youngsters. The latter had appeared in court on various charges other than scheduled offences and had also been admitted to the assessment centre for a short period. The main aim of the study was to ascertain whether the scheduled offenders constituted a distinct population which could readily be identified as different from the traditional social delinquents or if they were a group of people who would have been in trouble with the law in any case due to involvement in petty crime.

Boyle, Chesney and Hadden (1976) studied the backgrounds and previous criminal records of 476 defendants who came before the courts on terrorist charges. The authors were concerned with whether or not it was possible to distinguish between convicted terrorists and persons convicted of ordinary criminal offences and who had appeared before Crown Courts in England and Wales. They found that it was not possible to differentiate between the two types of offenders on social class factors but that the terrorist offenders were younger than

*The authors acknowledge the co-operation of Mr Purdy, Principal, Lisnevin School, Newtownards in permitting the use of the information reported in this chapter and of the Northern Ireland Office in providing access to the boys' criminal records. The help of Dr Brian Greer, Department of Psychology, Queen's University Belfast in the statistical analyses is also acknowledged.

.e others — only 13 per cent of the Ulster sample were over 25 ompared with 50 per cent in England and Wales. They also found that out half of the terrorist offenders had not appeared in court on evious offences.

Overall the data led to inconclusive findings and suggested that there as considerable overlap between terrorist and other offenders. The thors suggested that those coming to the courts on terrorist charges e not essentially different from those who might have got into ouble in other ways in more peaceful times. However because of the oubles more of these young people are becoming involved in more rious charges.

There were forty-two scheduled offenders who had been admitted the assessment unit in the three years prior to the initiation of this udy. They were matched with a control group of forty-two other ffenders. Matching was achieved by selecting a control admitted to e unit immediately following the admission of a scheduled offender. he only factor which differentiated the two groups was the type of ffence. The offences committed by the scheduled group were as ollows: possession of fire arms; intimidation; arson; armed robbery; jackings; robbery with violence; causing explosion/possession of omb; attempted murder and aggravated burglary. Typical reason for ourt appearance for the control group included the following: school uancy; motoring offences; care orders; burglary; theft; rape/carnal nowledge and malicious damage. There were equal numbers of atholic and Protestant boys in the scheduled group. The control oup comprised fifteen Catholics and twenty-seven Protestants.

Findings

he mean age of the scheduled offenders was 16.3 years compared with 4.6 years for the controls. That is the scheduled offenders were gnificantly older ($p < 0.01$). Table 10.1 also gives the intelligence and tainment scores of the two groups. It may be seen that the scheduled fenders had a mean verbal IQ of 95.4 and the controls' mean verbal Q was 89.2. This difference did not reach significance at $p < 0.05$. he Performance IQ of the scheduled group was 95.7 and significantly gher ($p < 0.05$) than the controls' mean of 88.7.

Similarly the mean Full Scale IQs for the scheduled and control oups were 95.3 and 87.7 respectively with the scheduled group gnificantly superior ($p < 0.05$).

Further examination of Table 10.1 reveals that the reading and ithmetic ages of the scheduled offenders are superior to those of e controls. The scheduled group had a mean Burt word reading age of

Table 10.1
Mean age, IQs and attainment ages of the two groups of subjects

	Scheduled offenders		Controls		
	Mean	SD	Mean	SD	
Age	16.3	0.5	14.6	1.3	*
Verbal IQ	95.4	14.0	89.2	14.0	N
Performance IQ	95.7	14.4	88.7	14.6	*
Full scale IQ	95.3	13.3	87.7	14.0	*
Reading age	11.0	3.3	9.2	2.9	**
Arithmetic age	10.9	1.8	9.5	1.7	**

NS Not significant
*   Significant at P $<$ 0.05
** Significant at P $<$ 0.01

11.0 and the controls a reading age of 9.2. The difference was statistically significant (p $<$ 0.01). The corresponding Vernon arithmetic ages for the two groups were 10.9 and 9.5 respectively for scheduled offenders and controls with the former significantly superior to the latter (p $<$ 0.01). The Junior Eysenck Personality Inventory (Eysenck, 1965) was administered to eleven scheduled offenders and fifteen controls. Mean extraversion, neuroticism and lie scores are given in Table 10.2.

Table 10.2
Mean extraversion, neuroticism and lie scores of both groups of subject

	Scheduled offenders N = 11		Controls N = 15		
Extraversion	20.1	3.2	14.7	5.2	*
Neuroticism	13.1	5.2	13.6	5.7	N
Lie	2.6	2.3	3.4	1.8	N

The scheduled offenders had significantly higher extraversion scores than the controls (p $<$ 0.01), however there were no differences between the groups on the remaining two scales where mean scores fell within the average range.

Table 10.3 gives details of some of the environmental circumstances relating to both groups. It may be seen that there was no difference between the groups with regard to a delinquent example being set by other members of the family, whether siblings or parents. None in either group was illegitimate and a few (three scheduled, four controls) from each had been in residential care for a period. Exactly the same number in each group came from one parent families and the same number of subjects in each group had a parent with a recognised

Table 10.3

Some environmental characteristics of the scheduled offenders and delinquent subjects

	Scheduled offenders		Controls	
Delinquent example				
siblings	14		14	
parents	4		4	
Illegitimate	0		0	
Residential care	3		4	
One-parent families				
Father absent	6		6	
Father dead	6	15	4	15
Mother absent/dead	3		5	
Alcoholic father	2		3	
Alcoholic mother	2		1	
Social class				
III	8		15	
IV	8		9	
V	21		17	
NK	5		1	
Member of youth club	4		2	
Psychiatric illness in family	5		4	

erious drinking problem that was disturbing home life.

Social class figures were not available for all subjects. However from those that were one can see that parents in the skilled category were under-represented in the scheduled group. Chi square analysis revealed there was no significant difference between the groups. Half of the scheduled offenders and 41 per cent of the controls came from social class V. This is higher than those figures obtained by Boyle et al. (1976) who found that 35 per cent of the terrorists in their study came from social class V.

Table 10.3 indicates further similarities between the two groups. Only six boys in all had had contact with youth organisations and four scheduled offenders and five controls had experienced the presence of psychiatric illness in a member of the family.

Physical illness as a child and a history of accidental injuries tend to occur more frequently in delinquent populations compared with normal groups (West and Farrington, 1973). In so far as was possible, previous illnesses and accidents were retrospectively examined in this study. Figures in this case may well be an underestimation. Those obtained are given in Table 10.4.

The delinquents suffered more childhood illnesses and accidents than did the controls. However in neither case did this difference approach significance. Hospitalisation as a child occurred in approximately 6 per cent of cases and there was no difference between groups.

Table 10.4
Personal characteristics of the scheduled and control subjects

	Scheduled offenders	*Controls*	
Physical illness as child	3	9	
Accidents	2	5	
Hospitalisation	3	2	
Referred to child guidance clinic	6	15	*
Referred to educational psychologists	1	12	**
Solo offence	1	10	**
Truancy			
Primary	4	14	*
Secondary	22	33	*

The numbers in each group who were referred to child guidance clinics or the schools' psychological service are also given in Table 10.4. Six scheduled offenders were referred to a child guidance clinic and one to the schools' psychological service. The corresponding figures for the delinquent controls are 15 (36 per cent) and 12 (29 per cent). These differences between groups in referral to child psychiatrists and educational psychologists are both significant (p < 0.05) indicating a greater frequency of referral for the delinquent subjects.

Table 10.4 also gives the numbers of subjects in each group who committed their offence in the company of others or whilst alone. Only one of the scheduled group was charged with a solo offence compared with 10 in the control group, a difference which is significant (p < 0.01). Truancy from both primary and secondary schools is apparent in both groups. Four scheduled and 14 delinquent offenders had a record of truancy from primary school. The corresponding figures for secondary school truancy was 22 and 33. That is the delinquents had a greater record of truancy from both primary and secondary schools (p < 0.05).

The figures as presented in Table 10.4 prompted a reanalysis of the data so far reported. For example, the higher proportions of subjects in the control group who committed their offence while alone, together with the increased number of delinquents who had at some time required referral to child psychologists or educational psychologists may indicate a higher level of psychological disturbance in this group. That is the control group may have included some emotionally disturbed youngsters as well as some relatively normal children whom Rutter (1975) described as socialised delinquents. If this were the case then differences between the two groups may be more marked than would be the case if the two groups were more homogenous in nature. To test this hypothesis all the subjects who had at some stage been

eferred to a child psychiatrist or educational psychologist were
emoved from both groups and the data reanalysed on the other
ignificant variables of IQ, reading age and arithmetic age etc. Dif-
erences at the same level of significance as before were found between
he two groups. This would suggest that while the degree of psycho-
ogical disturbance is an important variable in distinguishing between
he scheduled offenders and the control group it is still possible to
istinguish between the remainder of the control group and the
cheduled offenders.

Using the same rationale the youngsters who had been in court
olely for school truancy were removed from the control group since it
vas possible that their inclusion may have accounted for the differences
n intelligence and attainment test scores between the groups. The data
vas reanalysed but no changes in the significance levels were obtained.
rom this it may be concluded that even when significant minorities
re excluded from the control group it is still possible to distinguish
etween the socialised delinquents and scheduled offenders.

revious offences

or 24 (57 per cent) of the scheduled offenders the present offence had
rompted their first appearance in court. Four had been charged for
he second time, 8 for the third and the remaining 6 were appearing in
ourt for at least their fourth offence. The controls showed a somewhat
ifferent pattern with 13 being first time offenders, 13 appearing for a
econd time, 7 on a third occasion and 9 who were appearing for at
ast a fourth offence. The predominance of first time offenders within
he scheduled group was significant ($p < 0.05$).

ourt decisions

wenty-nine of the scheduled offenders and 29 of the controls were on
emand while at the assessment centre. The court decisions given when
hey appeared in court on leaving the unit are given in Table 10.5. This
nformation was not available in the cases of seven scheduled offenders
nd two controls. The main difference in court placement for the two
roups is that borstal and prison sentences were given in six cases for
he scheduled group but not at all for the juvenile offenders. Further-
nore 6 of the controls had their cases adjourned — a policy often used
o allow proof of good intent. The difference in dealing with the two
roups was just significant.

Table 10.5

Subsequent placement of some of the scheduled
offenders and control groups

Placement	Scheduled offenders N = 22	Controls N = 27
Training school	8	12
Borstal	3	0
Prison	3	0
Probation	4	2
Supervision	1	3
Fit person order	2	4
Adjournment	1	6

Reconvictions

Some of the subjects in the groups were admitted to the assessment
unit between three and five years before this study was carried out.
Since the average length of stay was about five weeks it follows that
ample time has elapsed since they left the unit to allow examination of
their outcome with particular reference to reconviction rates. Twenty-
six of the scheduled offenders were reconvicted and 29 (69 per cent)
of the controls. These figures of approximately a two-third reconviction
rate are in keeping with those obtained in many studies using juvenile
delinquents as subjects (HMSO Report, 1972) and point to a further
similarity between scheduled and other offenders.

It was also possible to examine the number and type of reconvictions. The 26 scheduled reoffenders appeared in court on a total of
55 charges, that is a mean of 2.1, whereas the 29 controls who
reoffended appeared on 73 occasions, an average of 2.5 per person. The
difference between groups is even more apparent when the total
number of offences is counted. The above figures refer to one court
presentation for one offence or combination of offences committed
around the same time. However it often happens that when a youngster
appears in court he is charged with a number of offences with others
taken into consideration. When all these offences are included it is
evident that the 26 scheduled offenders were charged with 112 offences
and the 29 controls with 250. This can largely be explained in that
when a person is charged with, for example, an offence like burglary,
other incidents can also be included as separate charges. In addition a
single motoring offence may involve such charges as theft, driving
without licence, insurance or L-plates, together with perhaps careless or
dangerous driving. The above findings suggest that those charged with
scheduled offences have, in general, been involved in a different type of
activity from the controls and are to some extent in keeping with the

comments of Boyle et al. (1976) who claimed that because of the 'troubles' more ordinary young people are becoming involved with the law on much more serious charges. However these findings also suggest that there are many youngsters who carry out purely delinquent activities.

It was also possible to examine whether the reconvictions of both groups of subjects could be classified as scheduled offences or not. Thirteen of the 26 scheduled reoffenders committed further scheduled offences and the other half had been subsequently charged with non-scheduled offences. Similarly among the control group there were scheduled and non-scheduled offenders. Ten of the 29 reoffenders from the control group have since been charged with scheduled offences. This latest finding once again points to a similarity between the groups although in terms of 'severity' of offence it may be qualitatively judged that the offences of the scheduled group were regarded as more serious by magistrates and judges since 31 per cent of the total scheduled group have been given prison sentences compared with 17 per cent of the control subjects. The finding that 10 (24 per cent) of the control group have subsequently committed scheduled offences prompted a step-wise discriminant function analysis (Wilks' Lambda) in an attempt to identify distinguishing differences between the two groups which might have predictive value.

The main variables used in this analysis were: full scale IQ; performance IQ; reading age, arithmetic age; referral to child guidance clinics; referral to educational psychologist; truancy from primary school; truancy from secondary school; and solo offences. They were selected since significant differences between scheduled and control groups were originally obtained on all of them.

The entire scheduled offenders comprised one group for this analysis and 32 delinquents the second group. The 10 subjects excluded from this latter group were those youngsters who subsequently committed a scheduled offence. They made up a third group for the analysis so that the programme could then predict whether they fitted best into the scheduled or non-scheduled group according to the discriminant function coefficient.

Table 10.6
Discriminant analysis prediction results

Actual group			Predicted group		
			Group 1		Group 2
	N	N	%	N	%
Scheduled – Group 1	42	35	83.3%	7	16.7%
Control – Group 2	32	11	34.4%	21	65.6%
Query – Group 3	10	3	30%	7	70%

The results of this prediction are presented in Table 10.6. As can be seen 35 (83.3 per cent) of the scheduled group were correctly classified as belonging to Group 1 (scheduled offenders) and 21 (65.6 per cent) of the 32 controls were correctly classified as belonging to Group 2 (controls). Overall 75.7 per cent of known cases were correctly classified but there were more misclassifications among the controls than among the scheduled offenders.

Of the 10 subjects in the control group who subsequently became scheduled offenders, the programme placed 3 as belonging to Group 1 and 7 to Group 2. The overall results of the analysis indicates that the nine variables which were included account for one third of the difference between the two groups, a finding which is disappointingly low.

The analysis also gave some indication of the relative values of the discriminating variables and ranked them in the order in which they contributed most to the discriminant function. This order is as follows:

1 Referral to an educational psychologist
2 Reading age
3 Solo offences
4 Truancy from secondary school
5 Referral to child psychiatrist
6 Truancy from primary school
7 Performance IQ
8 Full scale IQ
9 Arithmetic age.

Variables 1 2 3 and 4 proved to have the most discriminating power, however all contributed at a significant level to the discriminant function.

Discussion and conclusions

Some salient features emerge from the findings of this study and merit further comment. In general the results indicate that both scheduled offenders and youngsters involved in delinquent activities come from the same environment and have similar family backgrounds. The significant differences between the two types of offenders relate mainly to personal characteristics. That is, scheduled offenders are more intelligent, have higher educational attainments, tend to be more socially outgoing, are unlikely to have shown problems in maladjustment necessitating referral to educational psychologists or child psychiatrists, are unlikely to have committed their offence whilst alone and are somewhat less likely to have had a history of school truancy.

The information regarding subsequent offences committed by both scheduled and non-scheduled offenders indicates that clear-cut distinctions between groups cannot be justified. Half of the scheduled group who reoffended committed delinquent-type offences and one-third of the delinquents committed scheduled offences. This finding is not in keeping with those of Boyle et al. (1976) who reported that the offenders in their study did not have existing criminal records. Indeed not only have the scheduled offenders committed offences since leaving the unit, half already had a history of offences before admission to the unit. Therefore similarities between groups are apparent with regard to previous and subsequent offences.

Taylor and Nelson (1977) have commented that '. . . teachers in training schools, and lawyers, for example, are often aware that political offenders frequently have no criminal record, come from impeccably "respectable" homes and do not believe they have done "wrong" — all factors distinguishing them from many of their "non-political" fellows in borstals or training schools' (p. 16). The findings of the present study do not confirm this in that half of the scheduled offenders had criminal records and came from the same backgrounds as the other offenders.

The tendency for the scheduled offenders to be older than the delinquents is in keeping with the findings of Boal, Doherty and Pringle (1974). They found that offences such as riotous and disorderly behaviour, those involving the use of weapons, and theft were more common among older juveniles whereas younger juveniles tended to be charged with offences such as burglary and handling stolen property. This may well account for the fact that some of the 'younger' delinquents in the present study eventually became scheduled offenders when they were older.

In general the results indicate that no clear cut distinction can be made between scheduled and other offenders. There is considerable overlap between the groups and the final conclusions suggest that comments like '. . . but for the troubles this young man would not have been in court' (Boyle et al., 1976) are not applicable in many of the cases.

11

Changes in the attitudes of young offenders in an integrated assessment centre

William H. Lockhart and Ruth Elliott*

When Lisnevin School opened in November 1973 it became the fifth training school in Northern Ireland. It represented a new departure in the training school system as for the first time young offenders from both sides of the Irish religious divide were brought together in the close living conditions of a residential setting. At this time sectarian violence in the community was still at its height and the intake was to be drawn mainly from areas which had known much trouble. These were the 'ghetto' areas of Belfast which as well as having a high level of delinquency also have a reputation for entrenched sectarian attitudes. Contact between children of different religion is minimal in these districts, with the youngsters coming from a home environment and education system which often fosters religious segregation.

There were those who questioned the feasibility of bringing young offenders of different religious faiths together in a training school setting. They felt that the ghetto mentality would persist and that there would be constant friction between the two religious groupings which would result in an atmosphere of tension and hostility.

These fears were soon allayed when the school became functional. It was noted that while new boys often showed a desire to affiliate with those of their own religion, with a corresponding suspicion of the other religion, they usually, within a space of two to three days, adapted to the prevailing ethos in the school and made friends regardless of religion. Sectarian hostility was minimal and it was a common observation that quite deep friendships were formed.

It was these subjective observations which prompted the present piece of research. The aim was to investigate these apparent changes

*The authors acknowledge the help and advice of Mr John O'Sullivan, Advisory Service Computer Centre, Queen's University Belfast and Dr Patrick Slater, Academic Department of Psychiatry, St George's Hospital Medical School London.

in attitude and to determine whether they were purely transitory or relatively enduring.

Jahoda and Harrison (1975) in a study of Catholic and Protestant primary school children from 'troubled' areas in Belfast compared with a control sample in Edinburgh showed that Belfast children had a high ethnocentrism from an early age. Religion played an important part in determining how various role figures such as 'policeman', 'soldier', 'Roman Catholic priest', and 'Protestant minister' were viewed. They further showed that this ethnocentrism increased with age. This paper led to the formulation of the first hypothesis.

H1   Prior to admission to Lisnevin Catholic and Protestant boys will construe significant role groups in a different manner.

The second hypothesis was based on observations of closer identification and a softening of social prejudices during the time in Lisnevin and was stated as follows:

H2   A five-week residential assessment period will result in Catholic and Protestant boys construing significant role groups in a closer manner.

As it was considered that such attitude changes might simply be a response to the prevailing social ethos at Lisnevin which would not endure when the boys returned to their respective segregated environments, the third hypothesis was:

H3   Five weeks after discharge Catholic and Protestant boys' perception of significant role groups will have reverted to an intermediate position between those of admission and discharge.

Grid technique

When it came to deciding on a way to test the hypotheses repertory grid technique seemed most suitable. It derives from the personal construct theory of the late George Kelly as elaborated in his book *The Psychology of Personal Constructs* (1955); it is extremely versatile and allows the experimenter to develop his own measures in a manner which can be individually tailored to fit the needs of the study. What was wanted was a measure which would monitor the social attitudes or beliefs of one group towards other groups in society and also be sensitive to relatively small changes in attitudes over a period of time. Grid technique has been used in this way in a number of studies, for example Orley (1976) used grids in a social anthropological study of how natives in Uganda construed mad people and epileptics in the community; while Norris (1977) used grids to look at the effects of custody for a period of two months in a detention centre on a group of young offenders.

It was decided to develop a specific form of grid in a pilot study. The elements to be used in the grid were chosen after discussion between the authors and represented role groups which would be familiar to the subjects; some of them it was thought would be salient in discriminating between the criterion groups while others would be of a more neutral nature. The element titles (which will be described later) were then written on separate 5 x 3 inch cards and presented to 16 boys of a similar status to the subjects in the main study using the familiar triadic method developed by Kelly (1955) to elicit constructs. Approximately ten constructs were elicited for each boy and these were then pooled and subjected to a rather crude item analysis. It soon became apparent that a number of construct themes did recur, for example 23 per cent of the constructs referred to violence or damage, 14 per cent were of an evaluative nature, 5 per cent had a sporting theme, etc. From this data it was possible to choose ten construct titles which encompassed most of the main themes elicited, where appropriate extra weight was given to the most commonly occurring themes, (e.g. two constructs were devoted to violence whereas only one was given to authority). Care was taken to use simple clearly understood language in the wording of the constructs. Results from the pilot study also suggested that the boys found it easier to rank order the elements than to use a rating scale. These results were in line with Salmon (1976) working with children and Barton et al. (1976) who used grids with people of below average intelligence. It was therefore decided to use ranking rather than rating for the grid in the main study. As a consequence of the pilot study a 15 element by 10 construct grid was developed. The elements are shown in Table 11.1 and represent the following groupings.

Group 1 refers to peers, taking into account religious membership; group 2 to various types of authority figures; group 3 to para-military organisations and group 4 to neutral or anchorage elements. The reason for the inclusion of group 4 elements was two-fold. Firstly by including some neutral elements it made the real purpose of the grid less obvious, and hance less threatening, as indeed did the inclusion of some of the authority elements in group 2. Secondly it was felt that neutral elements would act as a kind of anchor in the grid which would serve as reference points with which to compare the movement of other elements. It was argued that it was unlikely that the subjects' perception of say old ladies or disc jockeys would be much affected by a five-week assessment period in Lisnevin.

Table 11.1
Elements used in grid

Group 1	Boys like me	
	Protestant boys my own age	
	Catholic boys my own age	peers
	Protestant girls my own age	
	Catholic girls my own age	
Group 2	The police	
	The British Army	
	Teachers in schools	authority
	Staff in training schools	
	My parents	
Group 3	Members of the I.R.A.	
	Members of the U.V.F.	para-military
Group 4	Manchester United Football Team	
	Disc jockeys	neutral
	Old ladies	

Table 11.2
Constructs used in grid

1. Most likely to fight/be peaceful.
2. I like best/dislike most.
3. Most likely to be bossy/not to boss you.
4. I most like to be with/don't like to be with.
5. Most likely to cause damage/least likely to cause damage.
6. Most likely to help you when you need it/least likely to help you when you need it.
7. Most likely to enjoy doing the things I like/least likely to enjoy doing the things I like.
8. Most likely to break the law/least likely to break the law.
9. Most likely to take care of others/least likely to take care of others.
10. Most likely to enjoy life/least likely to enjoy life.

The constructs are shown in Table 11.2 in their order of presentation. They are titled to demonstrate their bi-polar aspect.

Subjects

Subjects for the study were the consecutive intake of boys into the assessment unit for the period January to March 1977. During this time approximately 50 boys were admitted to the unit but a number had to be omitted from the study either on the grounds of not being sufficiently literate to reliably identify the element cards or because incomplete data was obtained (usually because of difficulty in contacting them after the follow-up period). Eventually full data was available

for 37 boys, 26 Protestant and 11 Catholic; this religious ratio of
approximately 2:1 was in keeping with the normal intake statistics
taken over a much longer period. The average age of the subjects was
15; they were of low average intelligence with a mean IQ of 89. All the
boys had appeared before a juvenile court on charges ranging from non-
attendance at school to robbery with violence. All boys participated
voluntarily in the study. The boys came predominantly from housing
estates or inner city areas which are divided almost exclusively
according to religious affiliation.

Procedure

As soon as possible after admission to the unit (usually the first but
occasionally the second day) each boy was asked to complete a grid. He
was taken to a private room where it was explained to him that the test
was for research purposes only and would not be used for assessment.
Some minutes were spent getting to know the boy and reassuring him.
The 15 element title cards were then placed randomly on a table
before him and he was given some time to familiarise himself with the
cards. He was then asked 'Which of these groups of people is most
likely to fight?' When a card was designated it was removed and the
question repeated until all the cards were ranked for that construct.

The procedure was repeated for all the ten constructs resulting in a
15 element by 10 construct matrix or grid. Occasionally a subject
would become stuck in the ranking process, on these occasions it
usually helped to turn to the opposite pole of the construct and
rephrase the question recording the data accordingly, e.g., instead of
asking 'Who is most likely to fight?' the question would be changed to
'Who is the most likely to be peaceful?' The whole process normally
took between fifteen and twenty minutes.

The day before leaving Lisnevin, that is after a time lapse of five
weeks, the boy was again asked to complete the grid using the same
elements and constructs. After a further period of five weeks he was
once more contacted, usually at home or in one of the residential
training schools and asked to complete the same grid. This meant that
each boy completed the grid on three occasions, first on admission,
then five weeks later on leaving Lisnevin and again after a five week
follow-up period.

Analysis

The completed grids were punched onto data cards and submitted for analysis using three of the programs in Slater's Grid Analysis Package. The grids were sorted according to religion and occasion which meant six groups of grid; that is, Protestant boys occasion I, Catholic boys occasion I, Protestant boys II, Catholic boys II, Protestant boys III and Catholic boys III. Each group of grids was then analysed using the Series programme which produced a consensus grid for each group. Each consensus grid was in turn analysed using the Ingrid '72 programme which produced amongst other things a principal component analysis of the data. Finally a comparison between various pairs of the consensus grids was made using the Delta programme which shows the salient features of variation between two grids as well as providing the general degree of correlation between them. The Delta programme was most useful in producing information about differences between Protestant and Catholic consensus grids on each occasion of testing.

Results

Figures 11.1 and 11.2 represent the element plot in the first and second component space taken from the Ingrid '72 principal components analysis of the respective Protestant and Catholic consensus grids on occasion 1.

Figure 11.1
Protestant boys: Occasion I

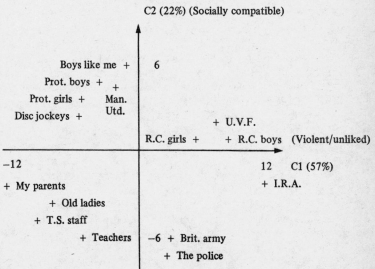

Figure 11.2
Catholic boys: Occasion I

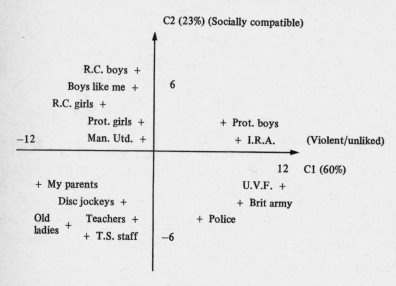

It will be seen that the grids are very similar. In fact it seems possible to designate the principal components by the same titles. These titles were decided from the weightings of the various constructs on the component concerned. For example component 1 which accounts for 57 per cent of the variance in the Protestant grid and 60 per cent in the Catholic grid is most heavily loaded on constructs 'likely to fight', 'likely to cause damage' and 'like best' and is therefore designated violent/disliked. While component 2 accounting for 22 per cent and 23 per cent of the variance respectively is most heavily weighted on constructs 'most like to be with' and 'likely to enjoy doing the things I like', and is labelled socially compatible.

The elements also show similar locations on both figures with a number of notable exceptions. Elements such as 'my parents', ' 'teachers', 'boys like me', bear very similar geographic locations, others such as 'the British army' and 'the police' lie in the same quadrant but have been displaced somewhat, they are, nonetheless, construed in essentially similar manners. Five of the elements, which might be described as the significant elements in distinguishing between grids, in fact, interchange their relative positions when the two grids are compared, thus the position occupied by the I.R.A. on the Protestant grid becomes the position where U.V.F. is located on the Catholic grid and vice versa.

Similarly the position occupied by 'Protestant boys' on the Protestant grid becomes the location for 'Catholic boys' on the Catholic grid and so on. The five significant elements are: 'Protestant boys', 'Catholic boys', 'Catholic girls', 'members of the U.V.F.' and 'members of the I.R.A.'. Protestant girls interestignly occupy a rather similar position on both grids.

The above results confirm hypothesis I that prior to admission Catholic and Protestant boys will construe significant role groups in a different manner.

Table 11.3 shows the results of a Delta analysis between Protestant and Catholic consensus grids on occasions I, II and III. The general degree of correlation is given first and then the correlation between each construct in turn.

It can be seen from the table that the general degree of correlation on occasion I was already quite high at 0.65 but that, in line with hypothesis 2 which implies that the construct systems of the two grids will become more alike after the five-week period of living together, the degree of correlation increases to 0.78. However, the general degree of correlation of 0.76 on occasion III scarcely supports hypothesis 3 that following discharge perceptions will revert to an intermediate position.

Table 11.3
Delta between Protestant and Catholic consensus grids

The constructs

Occasion	I	II	III
General degree of correlation	0.65	0.78	0.76
Construct correlation			
1. Likely to fight	0.92	0.90	0.95
2. Like best	0.14*	0.55*	0.60*
3. Likely to be bossy	0.90	0.91	0.94
4. Like to be with	0.36*	0.60*	0.62*
5. Likely to cause damage	0.93	0.94	0.88
6. Likely to help you	0.43*	0.51*	0.51*
7. Enjoy things I like	0.53*	0.86*	0.61*
8. Likely to break the law	0.87	0.88	0.88
9. Likely to take care of others	0.71	0.81	0.70
10. Likely to enjoy life	0.57	0.78	0.62

A closer look at the individual construct correlations in Table 11.3 reveals that while the two groups were remarkably high in agreement over the use of certain constructs, for example constructs 1, 3 and 5 they did show a considerable divergence on other constructs, notably construct 2 — 'like best', construct 4 — 'like to be with' and construct 6 — 'likely to help you'. These constructs are marked with an asterisk

in Table 11.5. It will be noted that in each case in keeping with
hypothesis 2 each correlation increases considerably between occasion
I and II. Once again hypothesis 3 is not confirmed.

The low construct correlations between the two groups on occasion
I can be explained in either of two ways. Construct 2 with a correlation
of 0.14 might suggest that the two groups understand the construct
'like best' in a very different manner, or more likely they do not differ
in their understanding of the construct but differ in the manner in
which they allocate the elements according to the construct, that is
they have the same understanding of what it is to like somebody but
differ in the people whom they like.

In fact, if one looks at Table 11.4 it becomes apparent that
differences between the consensus grids for the two groups are not
explained so much by a different understanding of the constructs but
more by different element allocation. That is, the elements vary, while
the construct meanings remain relatively stable. This is certainly the
common sense way of viewing the data.

Table 11.4
Delta between Protestant and Catholic consensus grids

The elements

Occasion	I	II	III
Elements			
Percentage variation			
Boys like me	0.8	2.6	1.6
Protestant boys	11.3	9.5	5.3
Catholic boys	20.0*	16.6*	15.0*
Protestant girls	2.5	1.4	4.0
Catholic girls	16.0*	12.9*	16.4*
The police	3.5	2.5	5.4
The British army	8.5	8.6	13.1
Teachers in schools	1.3	0.7	0.9
Staff in training			
School	2.0	3.4	2.9
My parents	0.8	2.0	2.4
Members of the I.R.A.	12.9*	21.7*	15.9*
Members of the U.V.F.	14.5*	4.7*	6.8*
Manchester United	3.2	9.0	3.1
Disc jockeys	0.6	2.8	4.5
Old ladies	2.2	1.7	2.6

It can be seen from the table that certain elements (those marked with
an asterisk) account for an unduly large part of the variation and may
thus be regarded as salient or significant elements in distinguishing
between the grids of Protestant and Catholic subjects. The elements are
those which might be expected from a knowledge of the social

attitudes in Northern Ireland, namely: 'Roman Catholic boys', 'Roman Catholic girls', and 'members of the U.V.F.', with 'members of the I.R.A.' and 'Protestant boys' also contributing considerably to the variation. These findings support hypothesis 1 that, prior to admission to Lisnevin, Catholic and Protestant boys will construe significant role groups in a different manner; other groups such as 'my parents', 'teachers' and 'the police' account for very little variation and are, in fact, viewed similarly. The data in Table 11.4 lends weight to hypothesis 2 but once again fails to confirm hypothesis three.

Before moving from Table 11.4 two other points must be mentioned. Note should be made of the element 'boys like me'. It can be seen that there is, in fact, very little variation on occasions I, II or III between the consensus grids for the two criterion groups for this element. This would suggest that while Protestant and Catholic boys view themselves as very different from each other they are in fact very similar, or at least they rate the element 'boys like me' as being alike on their respective grids. Thus the differences which they appear to see between Protestant and Catholic boys seem to be illusory or imaginary and are not borne out by their ratings of 'boys like me' or such constructs as 'likely to fight', 'likely to break the law', 'likely to cause damage', etc.

The second point is the change in percentage variation accounted for by the element 'members of the U.V.F.' which is large on occasion I and relatively small on occasions II and III. This point will be dealt with more fully presently.

The Ingrid '72 analysis produces a section of results entitled 'Distances between Elements'. Norris (1976) states that these distances may be regarded as an index of identification between elements, viz the lower the element distance the closer the degree of identification taken across all the constructs in the grid. In practical terms this means that an element distance of less than 0.8 units means close identification, a distance of around 1.0 (±0.2) is neutral and greater than 1.2 means lack of identification. Tables 11.5 and 11.6 represent the elements ranked according to their distance from the element 'boys like me', first for Protestant boys on occasions I, II and III and then for Catholic boys (in Table 11.6).

In Table 11.5 the mean change in rank for occasions I to II was 1.86 with a standard deviation of 1.87, the only elements with greater than one standard deviation change are marked with an asterisk in the table. It will be seen that only four elements do so. The U.V.F. starts with a rank of 4 on occasion I moves to a rank of 9 on II and further decreases to 11 on III. This would strongly suggest that during the five-week assessment period in Lisnevin Protestant boys began to identify themselves much less clearly with the U.V.F. This change was maintained during the five-week follow-up period.

Table 11.5
Protestant boys: ranked element distances from 'boys like me'

Occasion	I	II	III
Protestant boys	1	1	1
Protestant girls	2	2	2
Manchester United	3	5	5
The U.V.F.	4*	9*	11*
Catholic girls	5	4	4
Disc jockeys	6*	11*	7*
Catholic boys	7*	3*	3*
The British army	8	8	9
Teachers in schools	9	7	8
Staff in training schools	10*	6*	6*
My parents	11	10	10
Old ladies	12	13	12
The police	13	12	13
The I.R.A.	14	14	14

Table 11.6
Catholic boys: ranked element distances from 'boys like me'

Occasion	I	II	III
Catholic boys	1	2	2
Catholic girls	2	3	4
Protestant girls	3*	1*	3*
Protestant boys	4*	4*	1*
Manchester United	5	5	5
Teachers in schools	6	7	7
Disc jockeys	7*	9*	8*
The I.R.A.	8*	8*	6*
Staff in training schools	9*	6*	9*
The police	10	11	11
Old ladies	11	12	13
My parents	12	13	12
The British army	13*	10*	10*
The U.V.F.	14	14	14

'Disc jockeys' moved from a rank of 6 on occasion I to a rank of 11 on II but reverted to 7 on III. This variation will be returned to in discussion. 'Roman Catholic boys' moved from a rank of 7 on occasion I to a rank of 3 on II, this position was maintained on occasion III. This confirms hypothesis 2 which would require closer identification for 'Roman Catholic boys' and 'boys like me' from occasions I to II. It does not confirm hypothesis 3 that an intermediate position would be returned to on occasion III.

The other element to change in ranking between occasions I and II was 'training school staff'. Prior to admission to Lisnevin boys would have had very little exposure to these staff and probably viewed them in a fairly stereotyped way. The five-week period spent with them resulted in closer identification. Such a result might well have been predicted by those aware of the life-style involved which encourages considerable staff/boy interaction.

Once again in Table 11.6 those rankings which changed by more than one standard deviation are marked with an asterisk. The results at first sight appear to be rather anomolous. 'Protestant boys' on occasion I were ranked 4 and were similarly ranked on II. On the surface this would suggest that no closer identification had occurred between 'boys like me' and 'Protestant boys' between the two occasions, however the raw data shows quite a large decrease in element distance which the use of rankings masks.

In fact all the peer group elements show closer identification with 'boys like me' from occasion I to occasion II and are very closely clustered in terms of the raw data, with a relatively large gap before the next two elements 'Manchester United' and 'Staff in training schools'. From the data on occasion II it would seem more reasonable to say that Roman Catholic boys are failing to discriminate between the peer elements 'Protestant boys'. 'Catholic boys', 'Protestant girls' and 'Catholic girls' on occasion II, whereas they did so on occasion I. A similar situation persists on occasion III, where in fact 'Protestant boys' are ranked 1 although little change occurred in raw data between occasions II and III.

The data in Table 11.6 are broadly speaking supportive of hypotheses 1 and 2 and fail to substantiate 3. It is, however, less clear than the corresponding data for the Protestant group, probably because the Catholic boys started with closer identification with their Protestant counterparts than vice-versa and therefore left little room for changes in rankings.

Discussion

Perhaps the saddest thing revealed in this study was that on admission Catholic and Protestant boys construed the element 'boys like me' so similarly yet showed considerable differences in how they construed the elements 'Roman Catholic boys' and 'Protestant boys'. If generalised to boys in the community this is a sad reflection on the social situation in Northern Ireland and suggests that boys who are essentially similar in their lives, aspirations, etc., view themselves as different and divided. It does, however, demonstrate that many of their supposed differences (that is across ten commonly used constructs) are in fact illusory and is in keeping with the observations of many that boys of both religions live very similar life-styles and have more things in common than those which divide.

A Society under stress

On the bright side the confirmation of the second hypothesis and the failure to confirm the third suggests that even within a relatively short period of exposure to each other attitudes can change and closer identification occur. Moreover the results indicate that such changes may be relatively enduring. Such results must support those who argue for integrated education and give hope to the organisers of community relations activities, such as holidays, play schemes, etc., which bring the young people of both communities together.

A more detailed study of the various tables in this paper will reveal a number of other interesting changes which have not been mentioned, for example in Table 11.6 the change in ranking of the 'British army' from occasion I to II. A point which is perhaps worth mentioning is the use of neutral or anchorage elements in the grid. It was expected that these elements would remain stable in their rankings across all occasions. This proved to be generally the case but some variation did occur for which it was difficult to account. For example in Table 11.5 th element 'disc jockeys' moved from rank 6 on occasion I to rank 11 on occasion II and back to 7 on the last occasion. This could have been the result of random fluctuation which could happen if the element was not in the focus of convenience of the constructs used and was therefore not very meaningful to the subjects in this context, or else it could represent an actual psychological change. During the period of the study a very disturbed boy was in the unit: he exhibited troublesome, aggressive behaviour and came to be strongly disliked by the other boys. He particularly niggled them by describing himself as a 'Disc jockey' and domineering the record player. This could mean that the element was not nearly so neutral as had been envisaged when the study was planned. The use of anchorage elements should be viewed with caution!

In conclusion, it would appear that the value of repertory grid technique has been demonstrated in a study of this nature. It has detected psychological changes which were predicted from subjective behavioural observation, and while quantifying these changes in a manner somewhat different from normal statistical techniques, it has thrown light in a meaningful way on how people construe significant others in their environment with a sensitivity which belies many more orthodox methods.

SECTION V

EXPERIMENTAL STUDIES OF YOUNG PEOPLE

12

The development of ethnic discrimination in children in Northern Ireland

Ed Cairns

The work reported here is a series of exploratory studies carried out over the last three years in an attempt to provide a basis for the measurement and thus the investigation of factors promoting the development of ethnic attitudes* among children in Northern Ireland. This investigation was undertaken for two reasons. First, it was felt that such information could be of value in long term attempts to ameliorate the group conflict in Northern Ireland by providing measures for evaluating such attempts and, secondly, because it could be of theoretical interest in that virtually no studies have been conducted on this topic in societies where intergroup hostility is so marked in the absence of obvious perceptual features distinguishing the groups.

To date almost all the relevant literature on this topic has been confined to work done in the United States on the development of racial attitudes. In this context the suggestion made by Goodman (1964) has been generally accepted (Proshansky, 1966; Harding et al., 1969; Milner, 1975) that the development of ethnic attitudes is a gradual and continuous process which consists of three overlapping stages: ethnic awareness, ethnic orientation and ethnic attitude. Put simply, it has been suggested that ethnic awareness develops at an early age (about 3 years) and during this stage the child learns to perceive and label racial differences; in the second stage the conceptual nature of these labels is grasped, and in the final stage ethnic prejudice in its adult form emerges.

Recently however the many studies on which these generalisations are based have been criticised on several counts. For example, Brand

---

*The use of the term *ethnic* here should not be taken as an implication that the conflict in Northern Ireland is in any sense racial. Instead the term is used following Harding et al. (1969) to refer to any group who have in common one or more of the characteristics, religion, race, national origin or language and cultural traditions.

et al. (1974) have pointed out than many investigators failed to establish the subject's ability to discriminate the ethnicity of the stimuli before obtaining preference measures. Katz (1973) has also been critical of the 'core' studies, commenting that they have often done little more than demonstrate that children are not colour blind. In her work she has been particularly anxious to stress the role of 'perceptual categorisation' or 'perceptual differentiation', which she notes some investigators feel may be an aid to if not a prerequisite to the development of ethnic attitudes.

Ethnic cues in Northern Ireland

Before similar research with children in Northern Ireland could be undertaken it was necessary to obtain information on the methods used by adults to make ethnic discriminations. Therefore Lloyd (1976) asked a group of first year psychology students (N = 99), normally resident in Northern Ireland, to list as many cues as possible which are used in Northern Ireland to determine a person's denominational membership. Table 12.1 presents the five most frequently listed cues from each denomination. This suggests that both groups are in relative agreement as to the most important cues.

Table 12.1
Five most frequently listed cues

Cue	Catholic	Protestant
Area	63.4%	72.5%
School	75.5%	65.0%
Name*	53.6%	67.5%
Appearance†	43.8%	62.5%
Speech‡	34.2%	62.5%

* Includes first names and surnames
† Includes face, hair, eyes and dress
‡ Includes accent, content especially swear words

On the basis of these results it was decided to follow up the use of three of these cues, names, faces and accent. The work reported here is that based only on the use of names although tangential evidence has been reported concerned with accent (Cairns and Duriez, 1976) and preliminary data have been reported from a study which is underway investigating the use of faces as a cue to denominational membership in Northern Ireland (Stringer and Cairns, 1978).

Lloyd (1976) next asked a further group of subjects (N = 88) to list first names which they thought were 'most typical of' the following categories: Catholic boys' names, Catholic girls' names, Protestant boys' names and Protestant girls' names.

Table 12.2 presents the five most frequently mentioned names in each category. It was decided that these names would constitute the stimuli in future studies.

Table 12.2
Five names in each category most frequently listed by all subjects

Catholic				Protestant			
Male		*Female*		*Male*		*Female*	
Patrick	(84)*	Mary	(75)	William	(75)	Elizabeth	(43)
Sean	(83)	Bridget	(64)	John	(36)	Anne	(32)
Seamus	(66)	Bernadette	(51)	Robert	(33)	Susan	(25)
Michael	(41)	Therese	(43)	Samuel	(32)	Jane	(22)
Joseph	(28)	Patricia	(32)	George David	(27)	Joan	(20)

* Percentage subjects listing each name

Comparison with racial cues

Before proceeding to describe those studies it should be noted that information presented above is of particular importance because it emphasises a major difference between the basis for ethnic discrimination in the U.S.A. and in Northern Ireland. This difference revolves round the fact that discrimination in Northern Ireland is based not upon perceptual cues but upon stereotyped cues. That is, the features which distinguish black from white are in the majority of cases obvious and therefore agreed upon by all observers. The name cues in Northern Ireland however are not agreed by all and thus are in fact stereotypes, that is, oversimplified generalisations or beliefs (Krech et al., 1962; Brigham, 1971).

In this case the framework or model suggested by LeVine and Campbell (1972) for the way in which the perception of outgroup attributes is regulated proves useful.

$$ {}_{S}E_{R} = V \times D \times K \times H $$

Likelihood of response	Stimulus intensity	Drive	Incentive value	Habitualisation familiarity

Response strength   Intrapsychic determinants

This model allows for the fact that the 'perception' of ethnic cues in Northern Ireland is not based solely on physical stimuli (V) but is also determined by factors 'within' the individual (D, K and H).

This enables us to predict that, even if we hold V constant, wide individual differences in S^ER can still be expected. Particularly important in the context of the investigations to be reported here, this also suggests that one might expect children to take a longer time to learn to respond to Northern Irish ethnic cues than to racial cues. This is not only because the cues are more subtle but also because a response depends upon D and particularly K and H, both of which one might hypothesise would be lower in children than in adults. Finally one would expect D, K and H to vary with changes in demographic variables especially area of residence. Undoubtedly the intensity of ethnic feelings vary from area to area in Northern Ireland, related for example to the degree of integration of the two groups and/or the history of hostilities between neighbourhoods.

Adults' ethnic discrimination of names

Before any reliance could be placed upon developmental investigations using the names noted above as ethnic stimuli it was necessary to check with other adult samples that these names are indeed usually categorised in terms of their respective ethnic groups. In one study subjects (N = 40) were presented with a subset of the names, two from each category male Catholic, female Catholic, male Protestant and female Protestant (O'Neill, 1978). This reduction in the number of names was necessary because all possible pairs of the eight names were presented to each subject (a total of 28 pairs) who was asked to rate them on a five point scale from 'Very alike' to 'Very different'. The data from this exercise were then analysed using Kruskal's MD-SCAL programme to effect multi-dimensional scaling. Figure 12.1 represents the two dimensional solution produced in this way (stress value 0.60), in which the vertical axis clearly represents ethnic group and the horizontal is a less clear dimension but probably represents sex.

In a second study subjects (N = 192) were presented with four names from each category noted above plus four male 'foreign' names (e.g. Hans, Illya) and four female 'foreign' names (e.g. Blodwyn, Gretel) to make a total of 24 names (Cairns and Mercer, 1977). Each name was rated on a six point scale from 'Very definitely Catholic' to 'Very definitely Protestant'. Factor analysis of the resulting scores provided a four factor oblique solution with two factors loading on the 'foreign' names, another factor loading on the Protestant names, and the

Figure 12.1
Two dimensional solution for adults

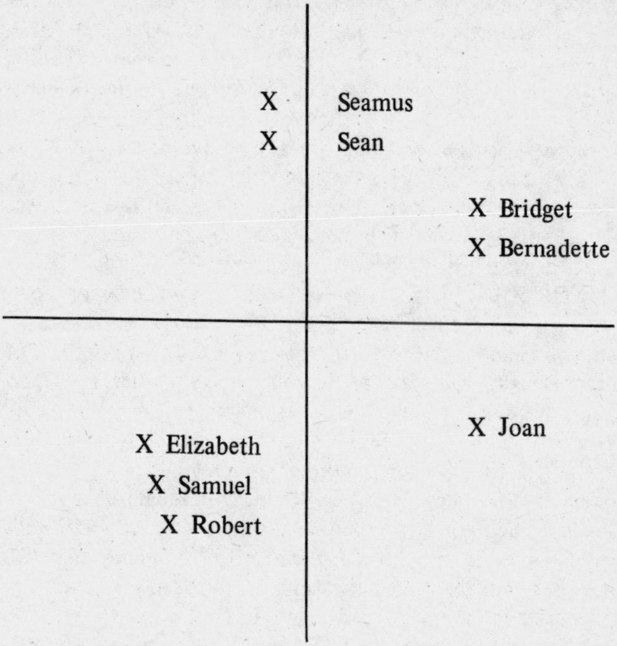

emaining factor on the Catholic names. Thus both of these studies uggest that adults in Northern Ireland do discriminate between this et of names on an ethnic basis.

Children's ethnic discrimination of names

Unfortunately the apparently simple next step of asking children in Northern Ireland to categorise names as Catholic or Protestant presents several problems. The most important of these problems is an ethical one. Because young children may not actually be aware of the use of names as ethnic cues it is possible that the very act of interrogating them on this subject may serve to sensitise them to this use of names. This means that a disguised approach is required in which it is not necessary to stress the denominational basis of the stimuli. Multi-dimensional scaling, as described earlier, would appear to be such a technique. Eleven- and eight-year-old Protestant children (N = 20) from a predominantly Protestant area and all attending the same Protestant school were tested in this way (O'Neill, 1978). The results, however, suggested that categorisation occurred only on the basis of sex, except for the male eleven-year-olds (N = 10) who apparently categorised in ethnic terms the male names only. Of course several objections can be raised to this study. Only two names from each category were used, and simply asking children to sort names is probably not a particularly motivating task.

A study by Cairns (1976) appears to have avoided some of these problems. In this study children's categorisation of the stereotyped names was assessed in the context of a free recall study. This was possible because it has been shown that when adults and older children recall a list of words they impose some form of organisation or clustering (Bousfield, 1953) upon the stimuli and the degree to which this clustering has occurred can be measured. This study made use of eight Catholic and eight Protestant names (with equal numbers of names representing each sex) plus eight 'foreign' names, included in an attempt to disguise the nature of the task and to control for familiarity. Further it is likely that the memory task increased motivation (D) to categorise, as this is one way to increase recall.

The names printed (in lower case letters) on separate cards were displayed on videotape and at the same time presented auditorally. Three trials were presented, each consisting of the names in a different random order with the added constraint that not more than two words from the same category occurred together. Each trial was followed by a two-minute recall session in which the children — all Protestants aged either seven years, nine years or eleven years (N = 21 in each case) — were required to write down the names they recalled. Testing was carried out in groups in the respective classrooms in a Protestant school situated in a predominantly Protestant town virtually free from sectarian violence during the last ten years.

Recall lists were scored to provide a measure of clustering in terms of the three categories present in each list — Catholic, Protestant and Foreign. Robinson's (1966) item clustering index (ICI) was calculated on each trial for each subject and submitted to a repeated measures analysis of variance with three between (Age) and three within (Trials) factors. This resulted in a main effect for Age, $F(2,60) = 6.23$, $P < .001$ and an Age × Trials interaction, $F(4,120) = 2.75, P < .05$. The mean ICI scores for each age group on each trial are displayed in Table 12.3. This reveals a definite increase in clustering with age (although preliminary work with adults N = 16 had indicated a mean ICI of 0.46 based on trial three readings only) and is in accord with other developmental investigations of category clustering (Neimark et al., 1971; Moely and Jeffrey, 1974) which have used a variety of stimuli and various measures of clustering.

Table 12.3
Item clustering index (ICI) at each age level on
each trial

Age (years)

		7	9	11	$\bar{X}$
T R I A L S	1	0.10	0.14	0.23	0.16
	2	0.11	0.12	0.16	0.13
	3	0.11	0.18	0.27	0.19
	$\bar{X}$	0.11	0.15	0.22	0.16

In order to examine the relationship between total recall and clustering (ICI) correlations were computed between these two measures separately for each age group on the final trial. This results in correlations of .07, (*N.S.*) .55 ($P < .05$) and 0.54 ($P < .05$) for the seven-, nine- eleven-year olds respectively.

Taken together, then, these results suggest that some clustering did occur at all age levels, that this was greatest for the eleven-year-olds and only for the nine- and eleven-year-olds did the clustering contribute to an increase in recall. If, as Jablonski (1974) has suggested, the age trend in clustering is indeed dependent upon an increasing perception by the children of the categories involved in each list then these results provide some limited evidence that at least the nine- and eleven-year-old children were aware of the ethnic nature of the names involved.

Yet the conclusions that can be reached from these data must remain somewhat limited. This is because, as noted above, LeVine and Campbell's model predicts individual differences in ethnic discrimination while the results presented above only provide information on group trends. Fortunately this problem can be overcome by using a measure of clustering (D) developed by Dalrymple-Alford (1970, 1971). This measure is based on the amount of clustering which actually occurred *minus* the amount of clustering expected to occur by chance. Thus when D is positive this indicates that for that individual on that trial clustering at above chance level occurred. Reanalysing Cairns' (1976) data using this measure it was therefore possible to calculate that 52, 55 and 76 per cent of the seven-, nine- and eleven-year-olds respectively showed clustering at a greater than chance level.

These results were confirmed by Barr (1977) who used the same stimuli and procedures as Cairns (1976) with both Protestant and Catholic children, this time living in a predominantly Catholic town, the scene of numerous sectarian incidents. Table 12.4 shows the frequency with which the children in these two groups clustered at greater than chance levels. The results from the Protestant group (see

Table 12.4) show a remarkable similarity to those obtained by Cairns (1976), noted above, and in fact are not significantly different (X^2 = 0.38, df = 2, NS), suggesting that minority group size does not effect the learning of ethnic discrimination in Northern Ireland. While the pattern obtained for the Catholic children by Barr (1977) is rather

Table 12.4
Percentage children showing clustering at above chance level at each
age group (from Barr, 1977)

	Age		
Denomination	*7 years*	*9 years*	*11 years*
Catholic	53% (N = 30)	60% (N = 25)	54% (N = 35)
Protestant	42% (N = 33)	53% (N = 34)	67% (N = 24)

different from that obtained from the Protestant group, particularly at the eleven-year-old level, the results are in fact not significantly different (X^2 = 3.02, df = 2, NS) suggesting that over this age range approximately equal numbers of Catholic and Protestant children tended to group these names into their ethnic categories in order to aid recall.

Therefore the results of these two studies (Cairns, 1976; Barr, 1977) suggest that while some children in Northern Ireland are capable of making ethnic discriminations based on first names, at least by age seven years, most children do not achieve this skill until age eleven years or older. These results also suggest that Catholic and Protestant children may not differ with regard to this ability nor is it influenced by demographic variables such as minority group size level of intergroup tension. Finally these results confirm that the development of ethnic discrimination is subject to wide individual differences.

Unfortunately pilot testing with younger children (five years) of the free recall technique scored for category clustering proved ineffectual. However it has been shown that 'recall by children as young as two years can be increased by the presence of categorical relationships in th to-be-learned lists' (Hagen et al., 1975) especially if the child is aware of the presence of these categories. Cairns (1977) attempted to manipulate children's awareness of the ethnic name categories by presenting the names in either random or blocked order to see if this would effect recall. This latter technique means that all names from th same category are presented together. Children aged five years (N = 40 attending either the Catholic or the Protestant school from which

rr's (1977) subjects had been drawn were seen individually, and
ter they had heard audio tapes consisting of eighteen of the names
ed by Cairns (1976) in either blocked or random order, they were
quired to recall as many names as possible on each of three trials.
nalysis of variance of total recall scores revealed no main effect due
 method of presentation (blocked v. random) $F(1,36) = 3.07$, NS.
milarly, total recall revealed no interactions either with the child's
nomination or the Name categories being recalled.

In a subsequent study Cairns (1978) gathered additional data in the
me way from older children, aged nine years, (N = 32) attending the
me separate schools (Catholic and Protestant) and also from two
oups of children, Catholic and Protestant, aged five years (N = 20)
d nine years (N = 36) attending the same school in another part of
rthern Ireland*. Separate analyses of total recall scores for each of
ese three groups (nine years separate schools, nine years same school,
e years same school) revealed no main effects for method of
esentation of the stimuli and only one interaction involving this
riable reached significance. This occurred in the analysis of the nine-
ar-olds at the separate school where method of presentation
teracted with denomination, $F(1,32) = 4.93$, $P < .05$. This indicated
endency for Protestant children's recall to be improved by blocked
esentation ($\overline{X} = 7.74$) compared to random presentation (6.55) but
 corresponding effect for Catholic children (7.66 and 7.07 for
cked and random respectively).

The accumulated results of these studies (Cairns, 1977; 1978)
ovide some evidence to suggest that children as young as five
ars do not discriminate among the names employed here on an
nic basis. Further these results suggest that separate schooling may
 this discrimination process, but only for older (nine-year-old)
otestant children.

Children's familiarity with stereotypic outgroup names

 the original study with five-year-olds which employed the blocked v.
dom design, Cairns (1977) drew attention to differential recall by
tholic and Protestant children of the Protestant, Catholic and foreign
muli employed. That is, a repeated measures analysis of variance of
 number of names recalled in each of the three categories in the list
atholic, Protestant and foreign) produced not only a main effect for
mes, due to the fact that fewer foreign names were recalled than

In the integrated school the ratio of Catholic to Protestants was 35:65,
pproximately that of the total population of Northern Ireland.

names from the other two categories, but, of more interest here, a names x denomination interaction also occurred, F (2,72) = 47.16, $P < .001$. Further analyses using Tukey's test revealed that this was due to Protestant children recalling significantly more Protestant names than *either* Catholic or foreign names and not recalling significantly more Catholic than foreign names. Catholic children behaved similarly in that they recalled more Catholic names than either Protestant or foreign but did recall more Protestant than foreign names.

Cairns (1977) suggested these results were due to familiarity. In other words each group was most familiar with its own group's names while Catholic children were rather more familiar with Protestant than with foreign names. Protestant children surprisingly were as unfamiliar with Catholic names as they were with foreign names. As Cairns (1977) noted, these results attest to the lack of intergroup contact in this part of Northern Ireland. The additional data gathered by Cairns (1978) noted above made it possible to examine the generality of these results at an older age level and also at both age levels (five and nine years) in both a segregated and an integrated school setting. Separate comparisons between the Catholic and Protestant children in each of the four groups (two at each age level at each of two types of school) revealed that, apart from the names x denomination interaction already noted, for the five-year-olds attending separate schools no other interactions emerged. Table 12.5 presents the appropriate means. Looking first at the effect of age, among the children attending the separate

Table 12.5
Number of names recalled in each category by Catholic and Protestant children at two age levels attending either a separate or an integrated school

School		Separate				Integrated		
Name category		P*	C	F		P	C	F
5 yr	Prot.	2.08	0.75	0.33	Prot.	2.00	0.60	0.30
	Cath.	1.50	3.08	0.18	Cath.	1.40	1.60	0.40
9 yr	Prot.	3.17	2.74	1.24	Prot.	3.62	2.94	0.62
	Cath.	2.91	3.52	0.94	Cath.	4.06	3.56	1.2.

*P = Protestant names
C = Catholic names
F = Foreign names

schools this shows that by nine years there is still a slight tendency to recall more ingroup names, but even for the Protestant children the ability to recall outgroup (i.e. Catholic) names has increased markedly.

ιe results from the integrated school are of particular interest. As
»ted above, the interaction between names and denomination is now
issing even at the five-year-old level. Examination of the means
veals that for the Protestant five-year-olds these are virtually identical
 those for the five-year-old Protestants attending the separate school;
e five-year-old Catholics attending the integrated school differ
»wever from those attending the separate school in that the former
oup shows no superiority of ingroup name recall (although the means
 the Protestant category are virtually identical regardless of school
tended). Finally the means from the nine-year-olds again show an
entical pattern for the Protestant children, regardless of the school
tended, while the Catholic children show a similar mean for their
group names but, if anything, an increase in the number of Protestant
ιmes recalled.

If differential familiarity is indeed the explanation for these results,
ιd it would appear to be the most parsimonious, then some interesting
ιough tentative) conclusions can be drawn. It would appear that
ost children in Northern Ireland (most attend separate schools) not
ιly do not learn to make ethnic discriminations, based on first
ιmes, at an early age but indeed by age five years are still relatively
ιfamiliar with the stereotypic names of the outgroup. By age nine,
»wever, this lack of familiarity has been overcome though it is
ιmpting to speculate that the early 'strangeness' of the outgroup names
ays a role in later development of discrimination and, as suggested
ν Allport (1958), also plays a role in the development of affective
hnic attitudes. The results from the integrated school suggest that
is pattern is not disturbed for the group which is in the majority
ιt that the minority group is in some way assimilated by the majority.
ιrther studies are obviously required to back up these ideas, based as
ey are upon limited data. However the results from the integrated
hool, at least, would appear to rule out one hypothesis — that
tegration of the ethnic groups in Northern Ireland would actually
ιd to a heightening of ethnic awareness and ethnic discrimination. In
is context of course it is probable that the proportions from each
oup play an important role as has been suggested in a racial context
ιmir, 1969).

Conclusions

ι the complete absence of information on the development of ethnic
ιscrimination in Northern Ireland the studies reported here were
ιsigned to be exploratory. In this sense they have made a substantial
ιntribution, indicating the various methodological problems to be
ιcountered in this area and suggesting solutions.

Yet the major contributions has not been a methodological one. Rather the most important outcome has been the highlighting of differences between the development of ethnic discrimination in Northern Ireland and racial discrimination in the U.S.A. Thus it has been shown that ethnic discrimination in Northern Ireland is based on stereotyped cues, unlike racial discrimination which involves the use of purely perceptual cues. This would suggest that the process should be more open to individual variation, and a model (LeVine and Campbell, 1972) has been noted which it is hoped will allow future studies to investigate the factors which may produce such individual variations.

Further it has been shown that the process of mastering ethnic discrimination probably takes a much longer time in Northern Ireland (about eleven years) than has been generally estimated for racial discrimination in the United States (about five years). This could suggest that racial discrimination and non-racial discrimination are radically different processes. However another possibility is that these two are similar but because of the obvious nature of racial cues the process simply takes a shorter time to complete. In other words the development of non-racial discrimination as noted in the studies reviewed here can be thought of as a 'slow-motion' version of the development of racially based discrimination. If this is so then it is probable that more is to be learnt from observing the development of non-racial ethnic discrimination where the process unfolds slowly, than observing the development of racial discrimination where stages are highly overlapped or may indeed occur in parallel. In fact the suggestio that with the development of racial discrimination stages may occur in parallel could account for the confusion in the literature when terms such as ethnic awareness, ethnic identity, ethnic evaluation and ethnic discrimination are used. Often it appears that investigators in the past have been tapping similar aspects of the problem but giving them the same name, and vice versa. Hence the criticisms noted above by Brand et al. (1974). Therefore racial attitude development in the U.S.A. may actually be a more complex process than generally accepted. Instead o the three stages suggested by Goodman (1964), Katz (1976) now proposes eight stages: (1) early observation of racial cues; (2) formatio of rudimentary concepts; (3) conceptual differentiation; (4) recognitic of the irrevocability of cues; (5) consolidation of group concepts; (6) perceptual elaboration; (7) cognitive elaboration and (8) attitude crystallisation. These stages, she suggests, span approximately the first ten years.

In this context it is important to recognise the need for cross-cultur replications of work done in the United States. Such data are unfortu- nately almost non-existent. Only one investigator has made a systemat attempt to study these problems and even this work had a racial basis, (Vaughan, 1963; 1964). Studying the development of ethnic awareness in White and Maori children in New Zealand, Vaughan (1963) suggested the importance of ethnic identification as a prerequisite for the development of ethnic awareness, which he suggested was not complete till age twelve. It is salutory to note that Vaughan's work has had virtually no impact upon the mainly American literature. It is possible that with some minor alterations (for example, deletion of stage 1) a combination of these models (Katz and Vaughan) will provide a better fit to the data which will be obtained from cultures such as Northern Ireland, where discrimination is not based upon obvious racial cues.

In conclusion the studies reviewed here are of importance for the general area of ethnic attitude development. Their importance for Northern Ireland lies in the caution they provide to resist the temptation to draw facile parallels between the Northern Ireland situation and the development of racial attitudes in the U.S.A. Indeed it may be that through studying the children of Northern Ireland more will be learnt about the basic processes underlying racial attitude development in the U.S.A. and elsewhere.

13

Pupil values as social indicators of intergroup differences in Northern Ireland

James McKernan*

The purpose of this paper is to describe a way of thinking about human values and value systems and a way of measuring values so that they may be widely utilised as social indicators of communal group differences and similarities. It is generally agreed that social indicators are measures of social conditions, e.g. health, education, unemployment, or individual differences (Rose, 1972). Social indicators are social yardsticks that make use of highly aggregated statistics that permit concise, comprehensive and balanced judgements about social phenomena.

It is widely believed that basic human values play an important part in shaping human behaviour. Thus human values might be considered as dynamic indicators of group differences. Unfortunately, quantitative information about the distribution of human values in Northern Ireland society is not available. Over the past fifty years, survey researchers have devoted considerably more attention to attitude and opinion research than to the empirical investigation of human values. This has been largely due to the fact that more sophisticated methods of measuring attitudes have evolved through the work of such men as Bogardus (1925, 1933) Thurstone (1931) and Likert (1932). The influence of attitude research has been reflected in recent studies into the Northern Ireland conflict. Studies by Rose (1971), Fraser (1973), Jahoda and Harrison (1975) and Russell (1975b) have concentrated upon beliefs, attitudes and reported behaviour of Northern Ireland respondents. These studies, however, make no systematic attempt to study a range of values held in Northern Ireland, or the relative importance of values to respondents. This latter task is a

* The author acknowledges the help and advice of Dr James L. Russell in the preparation of this chapter.

eneral aim of the research reported in this paper. More specifically,
he aims of this paper are to:

1 describe a theory and method of ranking human values according
  to their importance to individuals and groups;
2 describe the initial results of a survey of secondary pupils' values
  in Northern Ireland;
3 locate strong and significant differences between Protestants and
  Catholics and male and female pupils in the ranking of certain
  terminal and instrumental values; and
4 investigate, by step-wise multiple regression analysis, how
  intergroup differences in ranking terminal values of a political
  nature may be interpreted.

Theory

A value system may be referred to as an organisation of beliefs con-
erning preferable modes of conduct and end-states of existence desired
by individuals. There has been considerable disarray surrounding the
usefulness of the value concept as a guide to social and public policy,
nd how such a concept, if considered useful, could indeed be measured.
On both theoretical and practical grounds, the value concept could be
mployed as a key social indicator to provide guidelines to policy-
makers. For example, knowing how different groups accord importance
o certain values may shed light on particular problems in curriculum
development, in programmes of values education for instance. If
ducationists agree with Bernstein (1970) that it is important to reflect
ommunity values back to pupils, then they must begin by under-
tanding the values of their pupils' community.

In a signal contribution to the literature concerned with the nature
nd measurement of values, Rokeach (1973) has suggested two separate
kinds of values, called terminal and instrumental. The distinction
etween these sets of values is that they represent means and ends
espectively. Within a person's value system, instrumental values
means) refer to preferred modes of conduct and behaviour, e.g. being
honest, polite or obedient, while terminal values refer to desirable
nd-states of existence that people strive for e.g. equality, freedom and
alvation.

Subjects

he respondents purposively selected for this study consisted of all
ourth year second-level pupils (N = 751) present on the day of

interviews, attending schools associated with the Schools Cultural
Studies Project, a values education curriculum development project
based in the New University of Ulster.

Data was gathered from twelve second-level schools. The study
involved six controlled schools (N = 384) and six voluntary/maintained
schools (N = 367). In all, 315 females and 436 males in the fourth year
of secondary school completed the questionnaire. The achieved
population consisted of 51 per cent Protestants and 49 per cent
Catholics. While social class controls were not imposed, the population
was representative of working- and middle-class background, and the
respondents were drawn from areas near to and far from the border,
and from areas of severe political violence as well as areas of relative
peace and tranquility.

The survey was conducted in April and May, 1975. The study
included one grammar school, three comprehensive schools and eight
secondary intermediate schools in the counties of Antrim and
Londonderry. Fourth year pupils were selected because they were free
of the examination constraints of fifth year pupils and were felt to be
mature enough to grasp the significance and nature of the task.

Instrument

The Rokeach Value Survey instrument consists of two sets of eighteen
terminal and eighteen instrumental values. These values, accompanied
by a defining phrase, are shown in Tables 13.1 and 13.2.

The instrument employed in this study was Form E of the Value
Survey. In Form E respondents are presented with alphabetical lists of
eighteen terminal and eighteen instrumental values. Respondents are
asked to rank order the values 'in order of importance to you'.

The test retest reliabilities obtained for Form E are .74 for terminal
values and .70 for instrumental values (Feather, 1971).

Procedures

The author was present on all occassions to administer the survey
instrument to fourth year second-level classes, one class at a time.

Pupils were asked to study the lists of values carefully, and then to
place the number 1 beside the value that was most important to them;
then to place the number 2 next to the value which was second most
important. The value which was least important should be ranked 18.
Pupils were asked to work slowly and carefully, and were reminded
that the end result 'should show how you really feel'.

The average completion time was 20—25 minutes. No names were entered on the questionnaires, to ensure anonymity. No attempt was made to disguise the survey; it was presented as a Value Survey. In all, only three questionnaires were spoiled.

Mode of analysis

The cross-cultural comparisons were conducted using a series of programmes in accordance with SPSS (Nie, Bent and Hull, 1970). Because the frequency distributions deviated so markedly from one another, a circumstance to be expected with ranked data, the measure of central tendency considered most appropriate is the median, rather than the mean, and therefore the nonparametric Median Test (Siegel, 1956) was used as the main test of statistical significance. Secondly, in order to compare overall differences of groups in the relative importance of the values, Spearman rank order correlations (rho) were computed. A high value on *rho* indicates a high degree of similarity between value systems.

Finally, where highly significant differences existed in the ranking of certain terminal values ($P < .001$) between religious groups, step-wise multiple regression analysis was employed to determine which values accounted for the greatest amount of variance in the dependent variable. Using the SPSS programme of multiple regression analysis, all instrumental values were employed as independent variables.

Hypotheses

Three sets of predictions were made. In the first place it was expected that:

H_1 There would be a significant difference between religious groups in the ranking of the terminal values *a sense of accomplishment* and *salvation,* and the instrumental values *ambitious* and *forgiving.* Protestants will assign a higher rank to these values as they express the essence of the 'Protestant Ethic'.

Ho_1 There will be no significant difference between Protestants and Catholics in the ranking of the 'Protestant Ethic' values.

The above hypothesis was formulated in light of previous research by Lenski (1963) and Rokeach (1969, 1970a). Lenski argued that the values ambition and a sense of accomplishment come closest to the notion of the Protestant Ethic as expressed by Weber (1948). Rokeach has suggested that the two values salvation and forgiving stand alone as distinctively 'Christian' values.

Secondly, it was expected that:

H$_2$ There will be a greater difference between Protestants and
         Catholics in the ranking of instrumental values than in the
         ranking of terminal values.
Ho$_2$ There will be no significant difference in the ranking of
         instrumental values and terminal values between religious
         groups.

The above hypothesis was formulated on the premise that what
differentiates communal groups in Northern Ireland (as well as in other
cultures) is not so much their goals in life (terminal values) but rather,
their means of reaching these goals (instrumental values).

Finally, with regard to differences between the sexes, it was
predicted that the value systems of female pupils would differ
significantly from the value systems of male pupils.

H$_3$ There will be a significant difference between the sexes in the
         ranking of certain domestic values. Girls will place a higher
         value on *mature love, family security,* and on being *obedient*
         and *loving* than male pupils.
Ho$_3$ There will be no significant differences between the sexes in
         the ranking of the values *mature love, family security, obedien*
         and *loving.*

These hypotheses rest upon the assumption that women in Irish
Society are socialised into a domestic and subservient role which is
highly family and home-oriented.

Results

Tables 13.1 and 13.2 show the terminal and instrumental value medians
and composite rankings of values for the entire pupil survey (first two
columns). The measure of central tendency most appropriate with
ordered data, (18 point scale with different and unknown intervals
between specific values) the median, rather than the mean, was
employed to give an indication of how pupils as a whole ranked
specific values. The composite rank order was useful as a general index
of the relative position of particular values in the total hierarchy of
values, and elsewhere when comparing rank positions of particular
values across communal groups. Also included in the table are: (P) level
of significance, (as determined of chi-square median test) and
Spearman rank order correlations (rho).

   Among all pupils (N = 751), at the very top of the positive terminal
value hierarchy comes *a world at peace, freedom* and *happiness.* At the

Table 13.1
Terminal value medians and composite rank orders for Protestant and Catholic pupils in Northern Ireland

	All N = 751		Protestants 384		Catholics 367		P
rho = .94	Md.	Rnk.	Md.	Rnk.	Md.	Rnk.	
A comfortable life	8.3	(7)	8.1	(7)	8.6	(7)	.50
An exciting life	7.9	(6)	7.1	(6)	9.0	(8)	.01
A sense of accomplishment	12.7	(15)	13.0	(16)	12.4	(14)	.20
A world at peace	2.8	(1)	2.4	(1)	3.3	(2)	.05
A world of beauty	11.8	(14)	11.4	(12)	12.7	(15)	.01
Equality	9.7	(10)	11.2	(11)	7.9	(6)	.001
Family security	7.1	(5)	6.6	(5)	7.6	(5)	.10
Freedom	4.2	(2)	5.0	(3)	3.3	(1)	.001
Happiness	5.1	(3)	4.9	(2)	5.4	(3)	.20
Inner harmony	11.7	(13)	12.0	(13)	11.4	(13)	.20
Mature love	9.0	(8)	8.8	(8)	9.1	(9)	.90
National security	13.9	(18)	13.8	(18)	14.1	(18)	.90
Pleasure	9.7	(11)	9.7	(10)	9.7	(11)	.90
Salvation	13.2	(16)	13.0	(15)	13.5	(17)	.90
Self-respect	11.4	(12)	12.1	(14)	10.7	(12)	.01
Social recognition	13.4	(17)	13.5	(17)	13.2	(16)	.90
True friendship	6.5	(4)	6.3	(4)	6.7	(4)	.50
Wisdom	9.1	(9)	8.8	(9)	9.4	(10)	.50

Figures shown are the median; in parentheses, composite rank orders and the level of significance (P) for the Chi-square Median Test. Spearman rank order correlation coefficient (rho) used to compare value systems

bottom is *national security, social recognition* and *salvation*. This suggests that peace in Northern Ireland, and the world, is a leading value in the provision of freedom and happiness among school pupils in Northern Ireland.

At the top of the instrumental hierarchy of values are *honest, clean* and *loving,* and at the bottom, *logical, imaginative* and *intellectual.* The ideal of most pupils appears to be *a world at peace* where they are *free and happy* which is attained by *honesty, cleanliness* and *love.* This is a very idealised picture of end-states of existence and human actions. On the one hand, it underlines the idealism of youth, which should not be ignored by teachers, curriculum developers and all others with an educational responsibility. It provides a starting point from which educators can reflect pupil community interests back to pupils.

Table 13.2
Instrumental value medians and composite rank orders for Protestant
and Catholic pupils in Northern Ireland

rho = .95	All N = 751		Protestants 384		Catholics 367		
	Md.	Rnk.	Md.	Rnk.	Md.	Rnk.	P
Ambitious	7.2	(4)	7.5	(6)	7.0	(4)	.50
Broadminded	12.1	(15)	12.5	(15)	11.4	(15)	.20
Capable	10.3	(11)	10.2	(10)	10.4	(12)	.90
Cheerful	7.2	(5)	7.1	(4)	7.3	(6)	.80
Clean	5.5	(2)	5.2	(3)	5.9	(2)	.10
Courageous	10.7	(13)	10.5	(11)	10.9	(14)	.50
Forgiving	8.3	(8)	8.3	(8)	8.4	(7)	.90
Helpful	7.8	(7)	7.3	(5)	8.5	(8)	.02
Honest	3.8	(1)	3.5	(1)	4.1	(1)	.20
Imaginative	14.3	(17)	14.4	(17)	14.1	(17)	.20
Independent	10.9	(14)	11.2	(14)	10.6	(13)	.30
Intellectual	12.8	(16)	12.8	(16)	12.7	(16)	.90
Logical	15.2	(18)	15.4	(18)	14.9	(18)	.10
Loving	5.9	(3)	5.2	(2)	6.7	(3)	.001
Obedient	10.2	(10)	10.6	(13)	9.8	(10)	.20
Polite	10.4	(12)	10.5	(12)	10.2	(11)	.90
Responsible	7.6	(6)	8.0	(7)	7.3	(5)	.30
Self-controlled	9.0	(9)	9.6	(9)	8.5	(9)	.10

Figures shown are the median, in parenthesis; composite rank orders and the level
of significance (P) for the Chi-square Median Test. Spearman rank order
correlation coefficient (rho) used to compare value systems.

Protestant and Catholic sub samples

The religious factor is an independent variable which cannot be ignored
in any research into the values of pupils in Northern Ireland. Insofar
as religion is ascribed at birth, and insofar as the population of
Northern Ireland can be divided politically by religion, the chief
influence upon what is learned about many values may be decided by
birth into Protestant or Catholic communal groups. One would expect,
therefore, to find some differences between religions in the ranking of
values.

Table 13.1 shows that both Protestant and Catholic pupils rank the
terminal values of a *world at peace, freedom* and *happiness* either first,
second or third, and that neither group seems to care much about
salvation, social recognition or *national security*. For pupils of different
religious groups, (Catholics, N = 367, Protestants, N = 389) the rho
correlation between terminal values was .94. This suggests that the
terminal value systems of Catholics and Protestants are highly similar.

The results show that Protestants and Catholics do not differ significantly in their ranking of twelve of the eighteen terminal values.

With reference to instrumental values, the rank order correlation for Catholics and Protestants was .95, indicating highly similar value systems. The groups differed significantly (P < .05) on the ranking of only two values: Protestants placed a higher value on being *helpful* (P < .02) and *loving* (P < .001).

There are two terminal values on which Protestants and Catholics differ very significantly: (P < .001) *equality* and *freedom*. Rokeach (1973) has reported that equality is a value that has time and time again been found to differentiate between ideological positions. For example, American blacks rank *equality* far higher than American whites. Table 13.3 compares Protestant and Catholic pupils by whether or not they ranked *equality* above or below the median for the general sample. Catholics, as one might expect, rank *equality* more highly than Protestants. Catholics are 20 per cent more likely to place their ranking of *equality* above the median than Protestants. Of all thirty-six values, *equality* shows the greatest difference between Protestants and Catholics.

Table 13.3
Ranking of equality by religion of pupils in N. Ireland

	Protestant %	Catholic %
	N = (384)	N = (367)
Rank equality Above the median	(174) 45%	(235) 64%
Rank equality Below the median	(210) 55%	(132) 36%

Corrected Chi-square = 25.8 with 1 degree of freedom (.001)

In order to gain further understanding of why Protestants and Catholics rank *equality* differently this value was submitted, for both religions respectively, to step-wise multiple regression analysis using *all* instrumental values as independent variables. The instrumental values *cheerfulness, obedience* and *honesty* explained most of the variance in the ranking of *equality*, but these modes of action are difficult to interpret, and may not increase our understanding of intergroup differences.

Table 13.4 shows how Protestants and Catholics rank the value *freedom*. Three-fifths of Catholics rank *freedom* above the median against just over two-fifths of Protestants. Of all thirty-six values, *freedom* shows the second greatest ranking difference.

Table 13.4
Ranking of freedom by religion of pupils in N. Ireland

	Protestant %	Catholic %
	N = (384)	N = (367)
Rank freedom Above the median	(172) 45%	(219) 60%
Rank freedom Below the median	(212) 55%	(148) 40%

Corrected Chi-square = 16.0 with 1 degree of freedom (.001)

The value *freedom* was submitted, for both religions separately, to step-wise multiple regression analysis with *all* instrumental values as independent variables. For both religious groups, freedom is best interpreted by reference to *independence,* which explains 42 per cent of all the variance in the ranking of *freedom* predicted by instrumental values. In both religious groups, it is the pupils who value *independence* highly who are also likely to place *freedom* high on their list of values.

Table 13.5
Terminal value medians and composite rank orders for Northern Ireland boys and girls

	Male		Female		
rho = .96 N = 751	436		315		P
A comfortable life	7.2	(5)	9.7	(8)	.001
An exciting life	7.6	(6)	8.2	(6)	.90
A sense of accomplishment	12.3	(15)	13.3	(17)	.01
A world at peace	3.2	(1)	2.3	(1)	.02
A world of beauty	11.1	(12)	12.3	(14)	.20
Equality	9.3	(9)	10.4	(11)	.10
Family security	7.9	(7)	6.8	(5)	.001
Freedom	3.7	(2)	4.9	(3)	.02
Happiness	5.9	(3)	4.1	(2)	.001
Inner harmony	12.5	(14)	11.1	(13)	.20
Mature love	8.3	(8)	10.1	(9)	.001
National security	14.0	(18)	13.9	(18)	.95
Pleasure	9.5	(11)	10.1	(10)	.50
Salvation	13.2	(16)	13.3	(16)	.95
Self respect	11.7	(13)	11.0	(12)	.20
Social recognition	13.7	(17)	13.0	(15)	.20
True friendship	7.2	(4)	5.8	(4)	.01
Wisdom	9.5	(10)	8.8	(7)	.20

Figures shown are median rankings and, in parentheses, composite rank orders and the level of significance (P) for the Chi-square Median Test. Spearman rank order correlation coefficient (rho) used to compare value systems.

Overall differences between the sexes

Table 13.5 sets out the terminal value systems of male (N = 436) and female (N = 315) pupils. The rank order correlation for terminal values was .96, suggesting highly similar value systems. Despite this high correlation, males and females differed significantly in the ranking of eight of the eighteen terminal values.

Both boys and girls rank *a world at peace, freedom* and *happiness* either first, second or third. By contrast, both groups placed lowest preference for *salvation, social recognition* and *national security*.

Boys placed a higher value than girls on *a comfortable life* (P < .001) and *mature love* (P < .001). On the other hand, girls thought it more important than boys to have *family security* (P < .001) and *happiness* (P < .001).

Table 13.6 shows instrumental value systems for boys and girls. The rank order correlation between boys and girls was .91. Boys and girls, despite the high correlation, differed on the ranking of eleven of eighteen values. Boys and girls felt it most important to be *honest* and *clean,* and least important to be *intellectual, imaginative* and *logical.*

Table 13.6
Instrumental value medians and composite rank orders for Northern Ireland boys and girls

rho = .91 N = 751	Male 436		Female 315		P
Ambitious	6.3	(3)	8.4	(8)	.01
Broadminded	11.5	(15)	12.8	(15)	.10
Capable	10.2	(10)	10.5	(12)	.90
Cheerful	7.4	(5)	6.9	(4)	.30
Clean	5.8	(2)	5.2	(3)	.20
Courageous	10.2	(11)	11.4	(14)	.02
Forgiving	9.5	(9)	7.5	(6)	.001
Helpful	8.2	(7)	7.3	(5)	.10
Honest	4.4	(1)	3.0	(1)	.001
Imaginative	13.8	(17)	14.9	(17)	.01
Independent	10.8	(13)	11.0	(13)	.95
Intellectual	12.3	(16)	13.3	(16)	.05
Logical	14.7	(18)	15.7	(18)	.01
Loving	6.4	(4)	5.2	(2)	.01
Obedient	10.8	(12)	9.5	(9)	.02
Polite	11.2	(14)	9.5	(10)	.01
Responsible	7.7	(6)	7.6	(7)	.98
Self-controlled	8.2	(8)	10.4	(11)	.001

Figures shown are median rankings and, in parentheses, composite rank orders, and the level of significance (P) for the Chi-square Median Test. Spearman rank order correlation coefficient (rho) used to compare value systems.

Discussion

The purpose of this paper was to investigate the value systems of
Northern Ireland second-level pupils, and to consider values as a vital
social indicator of communal group differences. In the limited space
available only those differences predicted in the introduction to this
paper, and those especially dramatic political differences will be
discussed.

Overall differences between religious groups

At the beginning of this paper, a number of hypotheses were formulated regarding intergroup differences in the ranking of human values.
Firstly, it was predicted that Protestant pupils would rank the
'Protestant Ethic' values of *a sense of accomplishment, salvation,
ambitious* and *forgiving,* significantly higher than Catholics, insofar as
these values express the true 'essence' of the Protestant Ethic. This
hypothesis is not supported by the data. The findings show that
Protestants and Catholics do not differ in the ranking of these values.
On the contrary, there is almost complete agreement between religious
groups in ranking these values. What is significant is the relatively low
status assigned to the values *a sense of accomplishment* and *salvation*
in a country where religion is celebrated with a fervour and frequency
found nowhere else in the United Kingdom. As Weber (1948) has
suggested, the religious motive in capitalism has diminished considerably since the Protestant Reformation, and therefore this finding
might suggest that religious orthodoxy has little influence upon secular
life.

Secondly, in accordance with the prediction that religious groups
would differ more significantly in their ranking of instrumental values,
rather than terminal values, the results indicated that this was not the
case. The assumption behind this hypothesis was that communal groups
would not differ so much in their desired goals and end-states in life
(terminal values) but rather, they would differ in the modes of
behaviour and means (instrumental values) used to attain these goals.
The data show that groups differ more in terms of their goals (terminal
values) than their modes of conduct (instrumental values). The
hypothesis is rejected in terms of the similarity of rank order
correlations and the number of significant differences in ranking
specific values.

Overall differences between the sexes

In accordance with the hypothesis that female pupils would place a
higher value on certain 'domestic' values than males, the results show
that females actually do believe that it is more important to attain
mature love, family security and to be *obedient* and *loving*. These
findings suggest that female pupils may be socialised into adopting a
subserviant role in Irish society, and underlines the importance of the
family-oriented role assigned to Irish girls.

Political differences

Finally, the greatest differences between Catholics and Protestants were
found in the ranking of the 'political values' *equality* and *freedom*.
Catholics placed a higher ranking on both values (P < .001). This
suggests that it is politics, rather than religion or other factors, which
best discriminates between communal groups in Northern Ireland. The
value *equality* may be interpreted in conflicting ways. Catholics may
be generally interested in sharing all things with others, including
Protestants. Alternatively, groups frequently make use of popular
political ideologies in order to legitimise their rule or struggle for
power. The Catholic pupils in this survey show what is common elsewhere — minority groups seeking at least equality in public services and,
not least, a share in political power.

Catholic pupils also placed a significantly higher rank on *freedom*
than Protestants. The most generally acceptable way of interpreting
freedom in the Western world is 'freedom under the commonly
accepted restraints of the law'. In Catholic housing territories in
Northern Ireland one often finds 'freedom' expressed differently on
gable-end slogans. 'Free all internees' is a demand associated with civil
disobedience against what is considered an unjust law. 'Ireland un-free
will never be at peace' suggests 'freedom' within commonly accepted
territorial boundaries within which Westminster rule holds no power.
Interpreted politically, 'freedom' through 'independence' can mean
different things to different citizens.

To what extent has the case been made that human values may be
considered as important 'social indicators' of intergroup differences?
The results of this inquiry have indicated significant similarities in
value systems for second-level pupils of mixed religious backgrounds
and different sexes. The analysis of pupil value systems warrants a
number of conclusions. First, a major finding is that Catholic and
Protestants and males and females share highly similar value systems.

The results illustrate greater consensus of value systems than differences across and between groups in Northern Ireland. Rho correlations indicate a high degree of concordance between contrasted groups in terms of value system similarity, although greater differences are found between males and females than between Catholics and Protestants. Secondly, the 'Protestant Ethic' values are not good discriminators of religious groups differences. Finally the data suggest that females may be socialised into accepting a 'family-oriented' and subserviant role that is consistent with the traditional role assigned to women in Irish society. However, the extent and nature of intergroup differences in Northern Ireland are not well known, and bear further investigation. It would be unfortunate if social researchers were to overlook the similarities between groups reported in this study.

In conclusion, the results of the research reported in this paper raise several fundamental questions. First, do the various value terms have the same meaning for Catholics as they do for Protestants? For example, communal groups may interpret the values *equality* and *freedom* in very different ways. Secondly, asking pupils to rank values without relating them to specific social, religious and political issues may pose severe problems of interpretation, understanding and comprehension for respondents and researchers. It may be necessary to expand the meaning of some of these values. This problem is an obvious area for further research.

The Rokeach Value Survey is very valuable insofar as it indicates which values, considered with other values, are most highly valued by different groups. The method opens up new areas for social inquiry and allows researchers to concentrate upon areas most salient to educational policy. Viewed in these terms, the method offers a new beginning, rather than a conclusion to value research into communal group differences in Northern Ireland.

14

Factors associated with the development of deviant attitudes in Northern Ireland schoolboys

J. Damian Curran, Edgar F. Jardine and Jeremy J. M. Harbison*

The effects of the Northern Ireland (N.I.) civil disturbances on the present and future behaviour of children and young people has been the subject of considerable publicity and speculation (c.f. Fraser, 1973) over the last decade. Surprisingly few studies of a formal scientific nature have been completed, however, which may enable an objective assessment to be made. This point has been emphasised by several critics (e.g. Taylor and Nelson, 1978).

Jahoda and Harrison (1975), in one of the very few controlled studies, reported that N.I. children demonstrate a knowledge of prejudice and an understanding of religious separation by six years of age. Many of the present findings, however, have emerged from survey research. Rose's (1971) large-scale study of social and political attitudes suggested that modelling of parental attitudes is potent in the formation of sectarian values. More recently Russell (1975a) reported evidence of an increasing acceptance of violence by teenage boys from both communities in the province. Fee (1977), in his extensive survey of reading and behaviour among eleven-year-old children, obtained ratings by teachers on the Rutter scale. His findings suggested that while Belfast children do not differ on the neurotic ratings from Isle of Wight children and are significantly less neurotic than Inner London children, Belfast children do score significantly higher on measures of anti-social behaviour than both the London and Isle of Wight samples. These findings would suggest that the effects of the civil disturbances are both widespread and complex.

Other than the study by Jahoda and Harrison, which used relatively small and selected groups, little comparison on psychological measures has been attempted between N.I. young people and their counterparts

*The authors acknowledge the valuable co-operation and assistance of the principals of the secondary schools involved in the collection of data for this study.

in other areas of the U.K. The present authors, previously dealing with young delinquent populations in the main, became particularly aware of the difficulties of comparing and contrasting delinquent samples with young people not offending in the community (or at least not caught offending!) and also young people in other regions of the U.K. Preliminary work has concentrated on the development of reliable and valid scales of deviance (Harbison et al., 1978). The present investigation extends the work reported earlier (Curran et al., 1977) into an examination of some factors, mainly environmental, which may be associated with the development of deviant attitudes in normal schoolboys. This study sets out to compare groups of male schoolboys in N.I. with similar groups from other areas of the U.K. on standard measures of deviance and personality and attempts to identify some major variables which contribute to differences in attitudes shown by the groups. Obviously, the key to such a study is a reliable and valid measure of deviance and personality. From the research literature, the one selected was the Jesness Inventory (Jesness, 1966). This Inventory emerged as an empirical instrument from a large-scale research programme undertaken by the California Youth Authority during the 1960s. It is designed to classify delinquents and disturbed adolescents with the aim of using the typology to evaluate the effects of treatment on offenders. The Jesness Inventory was selected for the following major reasons:

(i) its proven validity in discriminating between delinquent and non-delinquent groups and in predicting future anti-social behaviour (see below);

(ii) its widespread use with English and Scottish as well as American normal and deviant groups aged twelve to twenty years (see below);

(iii) the ability to administer the test orally and thus avoid test problems with illiterate subjects;

(iv) the lack of relationship between the measure and I.Q.;

(v) its potential for testing groups of subjects.

To expand briefly on two of these points:

(i) Concerning validity, Saunders and Davies (1976), in a review of the use of the Jesness Inventory with British delinquents, concluded that '... there is now good evidence for suggesting that [four of the eleven scales derived from the Jesness Inventory] are related to deviant personality'. The present workers (Harbison et al., 1978) have extended this previous work on validity and demonstrated that the same four scales, plus a fifth not identified by Saunders and Davies, can differentiate between differing levels of delinquency in N.I. populations of normal children, delinquents and young offenders. These five scales are:

Social maladjustment: this refers to a set of attitudes associated with inadequate or disturbed socialisation as defined by the extent to which a youth shares the attitudes of persons who do not meet environmental demands in socially approved ways;

Value orientation: this refers to a tendency to hold values and report behaviour characteristic of certain class cultures — gang orientation, toughness ethic, fear of failure and the importance of luck and thrill in behaviour, along with a desire for early adulthood;

Alienation: this refers to the presence of distrust and estrangement in a persons' attitudes towards others, especially towards persons representing authority;

Manifest aggression: this refers to an awareness of unpleasant feelings especially of anger or frustration, a tendency to react readily with emotion, and perceived discomfort concerning the presence and control of these feelings;

Autism: this measures a tendency, in thinking and perceiving, to distort reality according to one's personal desires or needs.

(ii) Concerning usage, the Jesness Inventory, as well as being used extensively in the United States, has been employed with English Approved Schoolboys, Scottish Approved Schoolboys, boys in detention centres, young offenders on probation, Borstal inmates in England and English and Scottish boys in normal schools.

The inventory consists of 155 statements requiring either a 'true' or 'false' response. To overcome potential problems due to illiteracy, the test statements were administered to all boys in the present study by means of a cassette tape recording. The boys were tested in groups, usually in entire classes of twenty to thirty in their schools. Little difficulty, if any, was experienced by the subjects. This method of administration is accepted by Jesness as valid and has been used in most of the English studies where the degree of illiteracy is frequently a problem.

Three samples were selected for comparison:

(a) a sample of N.I. boys was selected from both controlled (or Protestant) and maintained (or Roman Catholic) secondary schools from a number of areas of Belfast and two smaller towns. A total of 961 boys was assessed, with ages ranging from 11 to 18 years and a mean age of 13.8 years. No attempt was made to exclude boys with a known criminal record.

(b) A group of 300 Scottish boys aged between 12 to 16 years, also with a mean age of 13.8 years. The sample of boys attended five corporation day schools in different areas of Glasgow, selected as representing the general social and economic background associated with higher incidence of juvenile offences in the city.

who collected this data, considers these boys as coming from schools which most adequately represent the general educational and social background of delinquents.

(c) The English sample, collected by Mott (1969), comprised 162 boys attending a comprehensive school. No selection criteria, other than age, were used to collect this sample which had a mean age of 14.2 years.

Results

Table 14.1 gives the comparisons between the samples from N.I., Scotland and England on the five selected scales of deviance.

Table 14.1
Comparative results of N.I., Scottish and English schoolboys on five scales of deviance

		Social maladjustment	Value orientation	Alienation	Manifest aggression	Autism
N.I. boys	M̄	24.3	18.7	11.7	17.0	9.3
n = 961	(SD)	(7.0)	(6.7)	(4.5)	(5.2)	(3.9)
Scottish boys*	M̄	23.7	17.9	12.5	15.5	8.5
n = 300	(SD)	(6.5)	(5.9)	(4.3)	(4.9)	(3.7)
English boys†	M̄	19.9	13.4	7.8	13.6	8.46
n = 162	(SD)	(6.1)	(5.5)	(3.5)	(4.8)	(3.3)

*Forrest (1978)
†Mott (1969)

On all scales — social maladjustment, value orientation, alienation, manifest aggression and autism — the differences between the N.I. group and boys from England are highly significant ($p < .001$). The results show, however, that the Scottish boys also differ on four of the five scales from the English boys — only autism does not distinguish between the populations. When the N.I. sample is compared with the Scottish sample, the N.I. boys score significantly higher on three scales of deviance: value orientation, ($p < .05$), manifest aggression ($p < .001$) and autism ($.01 > p > .001$). The Scottish sample obtains a higher score on alienation ($.01 > p > .001$).

These findings mirror information collected on delinquents and young offenders cross-culturally (Jardine et al., 1978) and suggest that both Scottish and N.I. young people express considerably more deviant attitudes than do English subjects of the same age. A contaminating factor here could be that the English data was obtained almost ten years ago and, in terms of cultural shifts and influences on young people's attitudes, ten years is a relatively long time.

The Scottish subjects were tested more recently, up to 1977. The findings show that Scottish and N.I. schoolboys share much more similar attitudes although statistically significant differences remain. This is particularly interesting since the Scottish sample consisted of 'five Glasgow Corporation day schools [which] were selected as most adequately representing the general educational and social background from which List D school children were drawn' (Forrest, 1978). Further, almost 17 per cent of the children in this sample had been detected, using Scottish Criminal Record Office information, as offenders. These were *not* deleted from the sample. In contrast, the N.I. boys were selected on the basis of providing a sample from a wide range of schools — city and small towns, inner city and suburban, controlled and maintained, as well as from both good and disadvantaged areas. The nature of the N.I. sample should therefore have been less extreme or deviant than the Scottish sample on the basis of present knowledge.

There is thus evidence that deviant attitudes and personality in N.I. young males may be more extreme than in the two comparative areas of the U.K. An attempt was then made to identify some of the factors implicated in this pattern of N.I. scores. The N.I. sample of boys had been selected to allow analysis of the effects of four major variables. The four variables studied were:

(i) Age: the age range of boys extended from 11 to 18 years;

(ii) Religion: of the total sample, 555 boys attended Protestant (controlled) schools and 406 Roman Catholic (maintained) schools;

(iii) Area: 425 of the boys lived within Belfast and 536 lived in smaller towns outside the city (one of the towns had a predominantly Protestant population, the other predominantly Catholic);

(iv) Status: 478 of the boys came from schools, either in Belfast or in the smaller towns, which could be defined as 'high risk' and the remainder of boys attended schools in Belfast and other towns which were classified as 'low risk'. Risk indicators or attributes of the school included truancy rate, delinquency rate, socio-economic status and general levels of community disorder in the catchment area which supplied the school with pupils.

A series of multi-variate analyses was completed to tease out those aspects of the variables, and the interactions between the variables, which were significant in producing higher deviance scoring. The analyses indicated an initial age effect whereby the younger boys in the age range 11 to 18 years (i.e. < 16 years) were significantly more extreme on the scales derived from the Jesness. As the sampling of 17- to 18-year-old boys was uneven across schools, and to allow comparison of boys of similar age across the three variables of Status, Area and Religion, 17- and 18-year-olds (N = 44) were excluded from the analyses, leaving a sample of 917 boys. Age comparisons were then made between those aged 11 to 13 years and those aged 14 to 16 years.

Table 14.2 shows the statistically significant effects (*p < .01) of the four variables on the five scales of deviance. For each significant effect the higher or more deviant score is obtained by the characteristic of the variable noted first e.g. Belfast boys are significantly more socially maladjusted than are boys from outside Belfast.

Table 14.2
The effects of age, area, status and religion on the five scales
of deviance

	SM	VO	AL	MA	AU
Age (11−13 years vs 14−16 years)				*	*
Area (Belfast vs non-Belfast)	*	*	*		
Status (high risk vs low risk)	*	*	*		
Religion (RC vs Protestant)	*	*			

Age is a significant factor in its own right with autism and manifest aggression only in this population, the younger boys obtaining significantly higher scores. Belfast boys are more deviant than non-Belfast boys in terms of social maladjustment, value orientation and alienation. Precisely the same effects are established for boys attending high risk schools, whether in Belfast or the smaller towns. Roman Catholic boys score significantly higher on the scales of social maladjustment, value orientation and manifest aggression than do Protestant boys.

A further analysis examined the relative potency of Status, Area and Religion on each of the 5 measures of deviant personality in terms of standard or T scores. The higher the T value, the more potent is the variable in influencing higher deviant scoring. It was found that Status tended to be more potent than Area which was, in turn, more potent than Religion on the measures of social maladjustment and value orientation. The results were reasonably consistent in indicating that Status and Area are the more influential although Religion has an exclusive effect on manifest aggression.

Some of these findings, and further analyses indicating quite complex interactions between Area and Religion, Status and Religion and Age and Religion in contributing more extreme deviance, were reported in an earlier paper (Curran et al., 1977). On the one hand, the results suggested that the age of the young person, aspects of the young people's environment (i.e. urban city *versus* small town, and risk status of the school) and apparently religious grouping were all significant. On the other hand, other recent work (Mercer, 1978) suggests that religion is *not* an important factor in the development of deviant attitudes. This, combined with the knowledge that in N.I. religion and socio-economic class are highly associated (Boyle, 1977), led us to try and examine other factors involved in the attitudinal variables measured. In addition to the information already collected (i.e. Age, Religious affiliation, Area and scores on the five valid scales of the Jesness Inventory), the following information was retrospectively available for all schools — and therefore all subjects:

(i)   pupil—teacher ratio;
(ii) size of schools;
(iii) average class size in schools;
(iv) percentage children receiving special educational help;
(v)   percentage children eligible and sitting C.S.E. and G.C.E. examinations;
(vi) percentage free school meals;
(vii) unjustified school non-attendance (i.e. the criterion was percentage children missing at least 25 per cent of the Spring term, 1977);
(viii) unjustified extreme non-attendance (i.e. the criterion was percentage children missing at least 50 per cent of the Spring term, 1977).

It is obvious that there are a number of inadequacies in this retrospective design in that much more selective information would be desirable, i.e. there are too few individual and family variables. These additional variables were studied, however, in order to examine in greater detail the earlier findings and because the results might generate further hypotheses which could be tested.

Table 14.3 displays the significant correlations found between each of the five scale measures of deviance and the various independent measures. The results indicate that the grographical position of the school (i.e. Belfast *versus* smaller towns), the individual child's age, the size of the school and the school's non-attendance record are the most important predictors of high scoring or deviant personality; religious affiliation, pupil—teacher ratio and examination success also have some significance, and the other measures bear little or no relationship. It is

Table 14.3

Significant associations between measures of deviance and other variables

	Age	Religion	Urban/ small town	Pupil/ teacher ratio	School size	Class size	% Children receiving sp.ed.help	% Sat exams	% Free school meals	% Unjust non-attendance	% Extreme non-attendance
SM		† *	‡ ‡	*	‡ ‡						
VO	†		‡ ‡	†	‡ ‡			*		†	
MA	†				‡			*		‡	
AU	‡		*	† ‡	† ‡			†	*	*	* *
AL			‡	†	‡					*	

*P < .05
†P < .01
‡P < .001

notable, however, that because of the large sample relatively low levels of association are required to produce statistically significant findings.

A further stage in this analysis involved an inter-correlation of the various independent measures or variables which showed (see Table 14.4) a number of large, internal associations indicating the interdependence of a number of the measures. This is due to the limited sample of schools. Schools with poor rates of attendance, for example, have a lower proportion of their pupils attempting examinations, have more pupils taking free school meals (i.e. poorer parents) and have more children in need of special educational help. Table 14.4 also suggests that certain key descriptive variables are contaminated by other more objective indices. 'Religion' has already been identified as such a potential label. A regression analysis was therefore completed to clarify the relationships between these variables. The findings suggested that, for the present sample of schools and pupils, 'religion' as a separate factor is more parsimoniously explained in terms of the strong link between 'religion' and, mainly, income levels (as measured by free school meal uptake). Likewise, 'status' is more parsimoniously explained on the basis of similar analysis and logic. Both variables were therefore eliminated from further analysis.

Finally, while Table 14.4 indicates that most of the independent variables are significantly correlated, it is valuable to determine the order of importance and the amount of variance in each of the scales of deviance that can be accounted for. The regression analysis completed on each of the five scales of deviance consistently indicates that, at most, 10 per cent of the variation in the individual scales can be accounted for by the independent variables. Table 14.5 shows the variance of each of the five scales that is explained and the most important independent factors in the analysis in order of magnitude.

Conclusion

The present study has shown that N.I. schoolboys express attitudes which are considerably more deviant and extreme than those found in England (or among the original American sample of children on whom the Inventory was standardised) when the five scales of the Jesness Inventory, identified as having most validity in N.I., are used. Comparisons with Scottish schoolboys provide broadly similar results. The Scottish sample of schoolboys was selected to be more 'at risk', in delinquency terms, by drawing upon Glasgow Corporation day schools — a fact substantiated by the presence of 17 per cent known delinquents in the sample. The N.I. sample, however, was selected to

Table 14.4
Inter-relationships of 'predictor' variables

Variable	% sitting examinations	% taking free school meals	Number of pupils for each teacher	% unjustified absentees	% extreme absentees	School size (number of pupils)
Association with area (high + = outside Belfast)	+ †					
Association with religion (high + = Protestant)		− *	+ †	− †		+ *
% needing special educational help	− †			+ *	+ *	
% sitting examinations in age range		− *	+ †	− ‡	− ‡	+ *
% taking free school meals (i.e. measure of low income)				+ *	+ ‡	− *
% unjustified absentees					+ ‡	− *
% extreme unjustified absentees						− *

Levels of significance: * P < 0.05
                      † P < 0.05
                      ‡ P < 0.01

Table 14.5
Predictors of deviance scales

Social maladjustment	Value orientation	Autism	Alienation	Manifest aggression
7.7%	7.6%	3.7%	8.8%	2.0%
City/small town	City/small town	Age	City/small town	Age
% receiving special education help	% receiving special educational help	Pupil–teacher ratio	% receiving special educational help	% sitting examinations in school
% persistent non-attenders	% persistent non-attenders		Class size	
Class size	Class size			
	Age		% free school meals	
			Age	

include an even distribution of schoolboys from both low risk and high risk schools controlled across area of residence (i.e. Belfast and smaller towns in the province). Nevertheless, the N.I. group scores significantly more extreme on three scales, i.e. value orientation, manifest aggression and autism. On the social maladjustment scale, the N.I. group mean score is the highest but not at a statistically significant level. The Scottish sample is significantly more extreme on the alienation scale.

These findings present interpretive difficulties. On the one hand, it may be argued that the high level of deviance in N.I. is situationally determined and that delinquency and deviance will recede as the civil disturbances decline. On the other hand, it may be argued that as the scales have been shown in other studies (e.g. Saunders and Davies, 1976) to predict delinquent behaviour in future, these comparative findings would then suggest that in some areas of N.I., when peace and stability return, problems of anti-social behaviour among the young may emerge and persist as a major feature of life. Some parallel may lie with the steep rise in juvenile crime in Britain during the war and post-war years which did not recede, relatively speaking, until the early 1950s. The factors held responsible (i.e. dislocation of social and family life, prolonged exposure to violence and its reinforcing effects) may broadly simulate, to some degree, the N.I. experience over the last decade.

Analysis of the effects of several variables implicated in the pattern of N.I. scores on the five scales of deviance indicates that area of residence (i.e. whether a young person lives in Belfast or not), risk status of the school, age of the young person and religious affiliation are significantly associated with higher deviance scoring. Further analyses of these factors show that status of the school and area of residence are the more potent variables in influencing higher deviance scoring and also suggest that religion may be peculiarly compounded by other social and economic factors in N.I. (c.f. report by Fair Employment Agency, 1978). The implications of these findings for social policy in N.I. may lend further emphasis to the concentration of more resources within areas of relative deprivation and the need to develop earlier preventative approaches to delinquency within communities and schools. The finding that age is a significant factor (i.e. the younger the boys the greater the tendency to deviance) is of particular concern.

At another level, the findings pose more questions than they seek to answer. It is paradoxical, for example, that the 'official' rate of delinquency in N.I. over the last fifteen years, in terms both of indictable offences known to the police and the proportion of juveniles found guilty before the courts, has consistently remained at two-thirds of the rate in England and Wales. While there is some evidence to suggest that young offenders convicted in N.I. are more delinquent than their counterparts in Scotland, England and Wales (Jardine, Curran and Harbison, 1978), the need for further research is indicated in the light of the present findings of higher deviance more generally in N.I. Two possibilities may, however, be considered: firstly, the incidence of 'dark' crime (i.e. unknown juvenile offending) in N.I. may be relatively excessive as detection and policing resources are diverted by the 'troubles'; secondly, while the proportion of juvenile crimes in N.I. is consistently smaller in relation to England and Wales, the 'official' figures are also indicative of a very steep rise in the rate of juvenile offending – the underlying factors responsible for this rise in juvenile crime in N.I. may not necessarily be the same as those in England and Wales (c.f. Ungoed-Thomas, 1972).

Further research is also indicated by the finding that only 10 per cent of the variation in each of the five scales of deviance is accounted for by the selected variables in this study. The present authors hope to develop and refine the measure of deviance, using statistical techniques and in association with researchers outside N.I., so that the understanding of the attitudes and behaviours being measured and of the factors involved in the development of deviant attitudes may be extended.

15

Some motivations of adolescent demonstrators in the Northern Ireland civil disturbances

G. William Mercer and Brendan Bunting*

The Northern Ireland civil disturbances which managed to kill 1,767 and injure 20,068 people between January 1969 and June 1977 (*Social Trends*, 1977), have been dragging painfully on for the past ten years or even the past four hundred years, depending upon one's perspective. For an equal length of time there has been heated rhetoric (but precious little data) concerning the motivations of the people who participate in these 'troubles'.

Mackenzie in his recent book *Political Identity* (1978) argues that the nineteenth century has bequeathed to us four types of political identity — nation, race, religion, and class. He believes that in present-day society the most powerful of these are nation and class. These concepts, he writes 'retain their power over all of us: . . . they cannot be thrown into a conversation anywhere in the Western world without (metaphorically) exploding it. They move men emotionally: a few of them they move to action' (pp. 148—9). Within the conflict in Northern Ireland they have indeed exercised their hold over men. No reviewer or observer of conflict in Northern Ireland can ignore them, indeed, the literature dealing with the conflict centres on the role of these powerful abstractions (Darby, 1976; Whyte, 1978).

The traditional political divide (in terms of political parties) has been between the Nationalists, with their emphasis on Irish Unity, and the Unionists, who have placed their emphasis on maintaining the link with Britain. The various Marxist interpretations of the present conflict are, of course, united in seeing the real conflict as one of social class. However, the bourgeoise is seen as having created an artificial division

*The authors acknowledge the advice and assistance of J. Beech, E. Cairns and J. Leslie, Department of Psychology, New University of Ulster, Coleraine in carrying out this research.

between workers based on sectarian lines. Therefore the stress in the various Marxist interpretations is usually on class and religion.

Social scientists have in the main addressed themselves to the social/ psychological differences between Protestants and Catholics. This religious divide is often seen as paralleling a racial/ethnic split in the society. In this case parallels are drawn between Blacks and Whites in America and Catholics and Protestants in Northern Ireland. From this viewpoint many of the same mechanisms are seen to be at work in the Northern Ireland situation as in situations of racial conflict. If these kinds of assumptions are made, then it would be easy for social scientists to transport readymade theories from America. Unfortunately it is hard to sustain a racial/ethnic argument (Stewart, 1977).

These various theories with their emphasis on nation, class, religion, and race make various assumptions about the underlying factors involved in the conflict. At a theoretical and macro level of analysis these assumptions may well be correct; however, it would be reasonable to suggest that those who participate in situations of potential conflict are acting out something that is important personally to them. So, for example, while at a theoretical or macro level of analysis it might be suggested that the conflict is one of class, if demonstrators do not perceive this as important to them, then one must question the motivation for the conflict. In short, these acts are performed by individuals, and their perceptions of who they are and of their motivations may well have some bearing on understanding the Northern Ireland situation.

Considering work dealing with the characteristics of those who have had contact with the civil disturbances, in a sample of 315 Northern Ireland university students Mercer, Bunting and Snook (1979) noted that Catholics reported more contacts than did Protestants, and that males reported more contacts than did females. In a second study involving 198 Northern Ireland university students, they reported that various kinds of contact (e.g. riot, bomb, being harassed) all inter-correlated positively and further, after comparing demonstrators with non-demonstrators using demographic, personality, social/psychological attitudinal and contact with the disturbances variables, suggested that contact with the 'troubles' could be conceptualised in terms of a positive feedback loop involving the perception of social powerlessness, combining with previous contacts to produce further contacts (Mercer, Bunting and Snook, 1978). They also noted that personality variables did not appear to significantly discriminate those who had been in demonstrations from those who had not.

It is the purpose of the present research to investigate the self-concept and motivations of a sample of Northern Ireland adolescents who have participated in demonstrations associated with the civil listurbances, in order to compare the various theories regarding the disturbances and possibly gain insight into some of their causes. It is the further purpose of this research to investigate the notion that contacts with the 'troubles' are patterned in the form of a self-perpetuating feedback loop, again in the hope of gaining insight into their causes and continuation.

Without formally postulating any hypotheses, the various theories and ideas concerning the motivations for demonstrations and confrontations lend themselves to certain expectations: if the demonstrators are motivated primarily by aspects of social class, then one might expect them to rank class more highly than do those who do not demonstrate, when responding to a hierarchy of self-perception items. If religion is a powerful motivator, then they could be expected to rank religion and/or religiosity higher than do non-demonstrators. If their motivation centres round making statements about their ethnic identity, then they would be expected to rank variables dealing with ethnicity more highly than do non-demonstrators. If their motivations are political, then variables tapping a political dimension should be ranked highly by the demonstrators. If their motivations involve out-group hostility, then they would be expected to be more ethnocentric than their non-demonstrating peers. If they are simply rowdies and thrill-seekers, then stimulus seeking would be expected to correlate with demonstration participation. And finally, if they are simply sociopolitical extremists, then a measure of liberalism-conservatism might differentiate the two groups.

It should be emphasised that it is not suggested that this research is making any 'critical tests' among the notions concerning the motivations for and causes of the civil disturbances, but rather it is simply attempting to understand how these behaviours are seen by those who actually participate in them.

Method

Subjects and questionnaire

A total of 369 male and 523 female Northern Ireland sixth form students (mean age 17.5 years), who were on a school sponsored tour of a Northern Ireland university, completed anonymous questionnaires containing the following items and measures: age; gender; self-concept and identity questions; questions on contact with the civil disturbances; attitudes toward the Northern Ireland situation; and attitudes toward protest behaviours as measured by Marsh's (1974) Protest Potential Scale. A sub-set of 146 males and 311 females also completed the

Wilson-Patterson Attitude Inventory (1975) which contains scales measuring Conservatism *vs* Liberalism, Realism *vs* Idealism, Militarism-Punitiveness, Anti-Hedonism, Ethnocentrism and Out-Group Hostility, and Religion-Puritanism. Also, a sub-set of 70 males and 257 females completed Zuckerman's (1975) Sensation Seeking Scale which measures Thrill and Adventure Seeking, Experience Seeking, Disinhibition, and Boredom Susceptibility.

Considering the self-concept and identity items in detail, the students were asked to respond to 18 items on self-concept, first in terms of a forced choice between two opposed concepts (e.g. I am happy/unhappy), and then in terms of rank-ordering the 18 pairs in terms of their importance to themselves. These pairs were chosen from a number of theoretical backgrounds: Jung (1964) suggested that the psyche can be plotted in terms of a Thinking *vs* Feeling dimension and a Factual-minded *vs* Intuitive-minded dimension, and thus these two pairs were included. Cattell, Eber and Tatsuoka (1970) note that personality can be thought of in terms of, among other things, extraversion, anxiety, and tough-minded *vs* tender-minded, and thus the items Shy *vs* Outgoing, Anxious *vs* Calm and Tender-Minded *vs* Tough-Minded were included. Mackenzie (1978) argues that major dimensions of identity involve aspects of nation, race, religion and class, and therefore Middle-Class *vs* Working-Class was included to tap class identity, Protestant *vs* Catholic was included to tap religious identity, both Unionist *vs* Nationalist and Republican *vs* Loyalist were included to tap political identity, and finally both Gael *vs* Planter and Celt *vs* Anglo-Saxon were included to tap ethnic identity. (It should be noted that Gaels were the original Catholic Irish, while Planters were largely Scottish Presbyterians who came to Ireland and set up 'plantations' some 400 years ago. The item Celt *vs* Anglo-Saxon makes a division between the Irish and Scottish Celts on the one hand and the English on the other. Finally, regarding political identity, Republicans and Nationalists tend to favour a united Ireland, while Unionists and Loyalists tend to favour the maintenance of the current political ties with Great Britain.)

Six other pairs were also included, at least in part in order to mask the more politically-oriented items: Young *vs* Old, Masculine *vs* Feminine, Passive *vs* Aggressive, Happy *vs* Unhappy, Intellectual *vs* Practical, Liberal-Minded *vs* Conservative-Minded, and Religious *vs* Not Religious.

The rationale for asking the students to rank-order these pairs was in order to assess the importance of these dimensions, irrespective of their content. In this manner it was hoped that one might be able to infer whether or not these demonstrations were motivated by class, religion and so on.

Contact with the civil disturbances was measured by asking whether
not the respondent had been in a demonstration, been present when
bomb exploded, been in a riot, been harassed due to the 'troubles',
en threatened due to the 'troubles', and/or had had close friends
jured due to the 'troubles'.

Attitudes concerning the civil disturbances were assessed by first
king the student how serious he/she thought the Northern Ireland
tuation to be in terms of a 6-point Likert-type scale running from
ot serious at all' to 'more than extremely serious'. The student was
en asked whether or not he/she felt that people would be justified to
tition, boycott, strike, occupy premises, destroy property and/or
e physical violence in order to improve the situation. These six items
ere then summed to form Marsh's (1974) Protest Potential scale,
hich is a measure of positive attitudes towards protest behaviours and
e tendency to condone violent means of social change. Finally,
titudes concerning how safe the student felt living in Northern
eland were measured by summing the responses to four questions,
ch measured using 6-point Likert-type scales running from 'very
fe' to 'extremely unsafe'. The questions involved the fear of being
ught in a bomb blast, the fear of being caught in an attack, the fear
an unclaimed box, and the fear of an unattended car in a 'control
ne'. The odd–even reliability of this scale was .63 in the current
mple, Spearman-Brown corrected.

Analyses

parate analyses for each gender were carried out due to the gender
fferences in contact with the Northern Ireland civil disturbances
hich have been previously noted (Mercer et al., 1978).

Initially the frequencies of the variables were examined and two
ere dropped due to lack of variance: Male *vs* Female (due to separate
alyses) and Riot Contact (less than 15 per cent indicated riot
ntact). Two-way analyses of variance were then carried out using
ligion (Protestant = 1; Catholic = 2) and Demonstration Contact
o = 1; yes = 2) on the remaining variables and all not showing a main
fect or interaction on Demonstration Contact at a $p < .01$ level or
tter were eliminated from further analyses. The rationale for
cluding religion in the analyses of variance was based on the finding
at Catholics report more contact with the civil disturbances than do
rotestants (Mercer et al.). A $p < .01$ significance level was chosen at
is point instead of the more usual $p < .05$ in order to eliminate
ssentially trivial relationships found at a $p < .05$ level in such a large
mple.

As there were no interactions found and thus one may assume linearity, zero-order correlations were used to describe the relationship between Demonstration Contact and the variables retained in the analyses.

Partial correlations and diagrammatic representations of some were then used in order to investigate the notion of feedback loops among the civil disturbance and Protest Potential variables. In more detail, the problem was to diagrammatically represent all of the significant relationships among these variables in order to locate their paths of influence. There were two criteria used to define a feedback loop: first, it must contain at least three elements which are significantly related in a loop fashion (e.g. A—B—C—A); and second that there is a sort of 'loose causality' as is an assumption in path analyses (Blalock, 1964) — that is, in the loop A—B—C—A, each point on the loop must arguably be able to cause the next. For example, Protest Potential would be unlikely to cause being in a bombing, while on the other hand, being in a bombing could cause an increase in Protest Potential. It follows that it is unlikely that Bomb Contact could be placed in a feedback loop, irrespective of its partial correlations. However, the combination of Friends Injured, Protest Potential and Demonstration Contact could conceivably form a legitimate feedback loop.

The procedure for plotting out the patterns from the partial correlation matrix is relatively straightforward: 1) find the highest partial correlation in the matrix, say A—B; 2) find the next highest partial correlation associated with either A or B, say C—A, giving C—A—B; 3) find the next highest associated with any of C, A, or B and so on. The pattern A—B—C—A would define an A—B—C loop, while D—A—B—C—A would define an A—B—C loop with a spur of D on A. Generally speaking, this technique will allow an extremely complex set of inter-relationships to be displayed in a diagrammatic manner convenient for interpretation.

Unfortunately, computer limitations would not allow a larger partial correlation matrix to be generated and so interpreted.

Results

Frequencies

Regarding the frequency of contact with the civil disturbances, the males reported more contact than did the females, and Catholics reported more contact than did the Protestants. Considering the males the sample consisted of 60 per cent Protestants and 40 per cent tholics, and of these 22 per cent of the Protestants and 47 per cent the Catholics indicated that they had been in a demonstration. The rallel figures for Harassed, Threatened, Friends Injured and Bomb •ntact are: 48 per cent Protestant and 71 per cent Catholic; 35 per nt Protestant and 52 per cent Catholic; 50 per cent Protestant and per cent Catholic; and 41 per cent Protestant and 65 per cent tholic. For the females a similar distribution occurred, with the nple consisting of 57 per cent Protestants and 43 per cent Catholics, d of these 16 per cent of the Protestants and 25 per cent of the tholics indicated that they had been to demonstrations. Again, the rallel figures for Harassed, Threatened, Friends Injured and Bomb •ntact are: 29 per cent Protestant and 43 per cent Catholic; 15 per nt Protestant and 32 per cent Catholic; 43 per cent Protestant and per cent Catholic; and 40 per cent Protestant and 51 per cent tholic. In all cases a chi-square test on religion by contact indicated tistical significance ($p < .01$).

alyses of variance

all cases of the Protestant/Catholic by Not Demonstrate/Demon- ate, there were no significant interactions ($p > .01$) between religion d Demonstration Contact. For both genders there were main effects < .01) for religion and Demonstration Contact on all of the civil turbance contact items. Demonstration Contact and religion also oduced main effects on Protest Potential for the males; however, ere was only a main effect from Demonstration Contact on Protest tential for the females. For males, there were also main effects < .01) for Demonstration Contact only on Happy *vs* Unhappy, iionist *vs* Nationalist Ordering (a political dimension, content free), publican *vs* Loyalist Ordering (another political dimension, content e), and on Intellectual *vs* Practical Ordering.

ro-order correlations

ie upper diagonal of Table 15.1 represents the zero-order (Pearson's correlations for the males among the variables retained in the alyses, as well as the means and standard deviations for these riables. The lower diagonal in Table 15.1 represents the same informa- n for the females. It must be remembered when interpreting the ree variables which were rank-ordered, that a low score on the variable ould mean that it has been ranked closer to 1, that is, higher in the -point hierarchy.

Table 15.1

Zero-rated correlations: males (n = 369) in upper diagonal; females (n = 523) in lower (decimals omitted)

	DC	BC	H	T	FI	PP	HU	IPO	UNO	RLO	PC	M	SD
Demonstration contact (DC)		38‡	41‡	36‡	37‡	54‡	13†	21‡	-25‡	-24‡	27‡	1.35	.53
Bomb contact (BC)	51‡		46‡	43‡	41‡	33‡	08	05	-10	-06	25‡	1.53	.55
Harassed (H)	58‡	51‡		66‡	50‡	40‡	06	07	-01	-01	24‡	1.61	.55
Threatened (T)	57‡	55‡	71‡		42‡	44‡	05	05	-07	-01	18‡	1.46	.55
Friends injured (FI)	53‡	50‡	53‡	54‡		43‡	-01	02	-13*	-15†	22‡	1.61	.54
Protest potential (PP)	73‡	56‡	59‡	64‡	55‡		01	15†	-14*	-15†	21‡	10.15	2.60
Happy/unhappy (HU)								12*	-03	-05	05	1.08	.28
Intellectual/Practical ordering (IPO)									-12*	-08	08	8.36	4.80
Unionist/Nationalist ordering (UNO)										69‡	-02	11.64	5.44
Republican/Loyalist ordering (RLO)											-01	11.21	6.26
Protestant/Catholic (PC)	12†	11†	15‡	23‡	15†	01						1.40	.49
Mean (M)	1.24	1.48	1.39	1.27	1.53	9.53					1.44		
Standard deviation (SD)	.56	.62	.61	.57	.62	3.22					.50		

Note: * = p < .05; † = p < .01; ‡ = p < .001

artial correlations

ıe upper diagonal in Table 15.2 represents the partial correlations ıong the civil disturbance contact items and Protest Potential for the ales in the sample, while the lower diagonal represents the same

Table 15.2

artial correlations: males (n = 369) in upper diagonal; females (n = 523) in lower (decimals omitted)

	DC	BC	H	T	FI	PP
emonstration contact (DC)		13*	10	01	13*	24‡
›mb contact (BC)	06		19‡	07	15†	−01
arassed (H)	14†	10*		51‡	22‡	01
areatened (T)	05	09*	43‡		04	10
iends injured (FI)	10*	15†	12†	11*		11*
otest potential (PP)	29‡	00	01	04	−01	

ɔte: * = $p < .05$; † = $p < .01$; ‡ = $p < .001$

ıformation for the females. Figure 15.1 diagrammatically represents, ɔr both genders, all of the $p < .05$ relationships among these variables y joining the related variables with straight lines. The arrow heads on ıese lines represent possible directions of influence. For example, the ɔuble arrow head between Demonstration Contact and Friends ajured argues that not only could the subject's friends being injured ue to the 'troubles' motivate him/her to demonstrate, but also that the ubject's friends could be injured in a demonstration in which the ubject also participated. On the other hand, being in a bombing could ause one to feel harassed, but feeling harassed would be unlikely to ause one to be in a bombing, thus the single-headed arrows from ᴋomb Contact.

Discussion

ıferring motivation to demonstrate from the data, the demonstrators ᴋrom both sexes appear to feel that protest behaviours are justifiable ıeans to improve the social situation, as Protest Potential correlated ɔositively with Demonstration Contact for each. The males only seem ɔolitically motivated, in as much as both Unionist/Nationalist Ordering ınd Republican/Loyalist Ordering correlated negatively (i.e. closer to ı ranking of 1) with Demonstration Contact. Also, for the males only, ıntellectual/Practical Ordering correlated positively (i.e. lower in the ıierarchy) with Demonstration Contact. The only explanation that can

Figure 15.1
Diagrammatic representation of statistically significant partial correlations

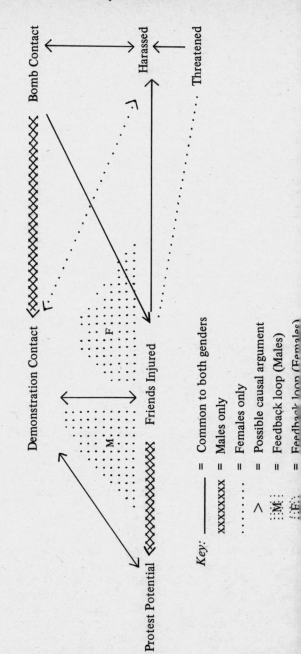

Key:

———	=	Common to both genders
xxxxxxxx	=	Males only
· · · · · ·	=	Females only
>	=	Possible causal argument
::M::	=	Feedback loop (Males)
::F::	=	Feedback loop (Females)

offered for this is that perhaps the demonstrators make little
tinction between the intellectual and the practical, seeing themselves
practically-oriented intellectuals who demonstrate for both motives,
d thus simply reject this dimension by ranking it lower than their
n-demonstrating peers. As to the positive correlation between seeing
mselves as unhappy and Demonstration Contact, it is a matter of
njecture as to whether or not these adolescent males demonstrate
cause they are unhappy, are unhappy because they do not like the
tcome of their demonstrations, or even both, as would be true if the
o were operating in a feedback-loop fashion. Finally, the fact that
litically-oriented variables predicted Demonstration Contact for the
les and not for the females may be in part due to basic gender
ferences in motivations and values (see Hutt, 1972, especially p.
0).

Turning to the question of whether or not the 'troubles' in part can
interpreted in terms of self-perpetuating positive feedback loops,
e evidence appears to be modestly affirmative. For the males, the
ument presented in Figure 15.1 suggests that having friends injured
e to the 'troubles' increases one's positive attitudes towards protest
haviours (Protest Potential), which in turn increases the probability
participating in a demonstration, during which one's friends could
injured and so on. Further, having been in a bombing increases the
obability of being in a demonstration and possibly having friends
ured in same, while being in a bombing, having one's friends injured,
d being threatened all increase feelings of harassment due to the
oubles'. For the females a similar pattern emerged, with Bomb
ntact, Friends Injured and Threatened all contributing to feeling
rassed and Bomb Contact also contributing to Friends Injured. On
e other hand, there appears to be a positive feedback loop for the
males among Demonstration Contact, Friends Injured and Harassed,
th Protest Potential not being included in a feedback loop but
netheless contributing to Demonstration Contact. Also, for the
males only, there is a statistically significant relationship between
ends Injured and Threatened; however no 'loose causal' argument
eing posited for this finding. It is noteworthy that having friends
ured due to the 'troubles' is a component in the loops for both
ders, and thus may be considered a substantial motivator for
monstration participation. Indeed, this was the initial motivation
the formation of the Peace People movement in Northern Ireland.
elfast Telegraph, 1976; Corrigan, 1976).

Finally, as has been noted before (Mercer et al., 1979), males
orted more contact with the 'troubles' than did females, and
tholics reported more contact than did Protestants.

A particularly interesting finding of the present research is, oddly enough, the lack of findings: religiosity, stimulus seeking, class, liberalism *vs* conservatism, ethnicity, ethnocentrism and so on all faile to discriminate the demonstrators from the non-demonstrators. Considering religion, certainly there are correlates between religious denomination and political views in Northern Ireland: in this sample 97 per cent of the Catholics indicated that they were Republicans and or Nationalists, while 81 per cent of the Protestants indicated that the were Unionists and/or Loyalists. However, it would appear that the motivations for participation in demonstrations for both denominatio are more political and/or social than religious. On the other hand, it c be useful for politicians to equate religion with politics, as in that manner they can acquire a loyal and reliable following and need never move from demagoguery to the more difficult business of statesman-ship. By the same token, a 'politics = religion' equation is probably simple and appealing to a large proportion of the population, as it put God on their side, the Devil on the other side, and can be used to justify almost anything.

While the present data suggest political and/or social motivations f the participation of adolescents in demonstrations in Northern Irelan and also that the 'troubles' can be seen as being in some ways their own cause and continuation, they are not necessarily the 'causes' of t civil disturbances. In point of fact, the whole notion of direct causalit may not be applicable to what could better be thought of as a comple and dysfunctional system of interactions, probably occurring on a number of social and interpersonal levels simultaneously. Consequent researchers should abandon the examination of bivariate relationships and 'independent' and 'dependent' variables and turn instead to the examination of patterns and interactions in order to begin to understand the Northern Ireland conflict.

SECTION VI
EPILOGUE

16

A place not so far apart: conclusions of an outsider

Halla Beloff

So what is special about this contribution to the river of words flowing over, under, and around the Northern Ireland problem? A psychology of Northern Ireland? Among all the 'models' for the inter-group hostility — Marxist, neo or traditional, political, historical, and indeed psychopathological (Whyte, 1978) — the social-psychological has not loomed large. A fitting modesty among social psychologists one might have said — but it is clear that these papers do make a special addition to the debate. Within the frame of the demographic and 'real life' evidence of stress, deprivation and coping, we can begin to have a new understanding of the form of the dissensus, its power and its limitation. Indeed no further argument for the modest, empirical stance of the psychologist is needed than the simple demonstration here made of the limits of conflict and the power of consensus.

In 1962 the two Quakers, Denis P. Barritt and Charles F. Carter, published a simple book, *The Northern Ireland Problem,* and brought an amazing breath of commonsense into the domain of prejudice study. Their plain description of the Ulster community showed that there was no necessary or interesting psycho-dynamic or pathological-need interpretation for a community that practised anti-locution, segregation, discrimination and many other manifestations of social prejudice on both parts of the group divide. They broke into the capsule of the psychology of prejudice and showed that open tradition and the learning of that tradition, coupled with economic deprivation could provide the motive power for a normal kind of prejudice.

If psychologists by this lesson and others (for example, that by the black student of racism, James Jones, 1972) have come away from a preoccupation with victimology and the labelling of deviant bigots to an understanding of the intrinsic web of cultural racism in our society, so now child psychologists and social psychologists may take courage of our Ulster colleagues here and come out from our laboratories and clinics to describe and explain normal adjustment to abnormal circumstances.

There is no question that there have been dramatic, not to say sensational, advances in child psychology in the last fifteen years. But these advances, led by such workers as Bruner (1968), Bower (1977) and Schaffer (1977) have been closely bounded within the domain of cognitive development, and have resulted most spectacularly in our being able to talk confidently about the competent *infant.*

That somehow still leaves children and young people out there on the street, in the pub and the disco — working out the world in a way we know little about. And it seems that the fruitful studies are being carried out by others — architects (Colin Ward, 1977) and, of course, sociologists (for example, Hall and Jefferson, 1977; Robins and Cohen, 1978). The strengths of these studies have been not only their intuitive insights, but the interpretation of options and the limitation of options which especially inform analyses in terms of the youth culture. And it is the salience of a political ideology in the works of the sociologists that enables them to make a bridge between society and the individual which brings alive their analyses of status, authority, class and intergroup comparison.

The present work demonstrates the beginning of another kind of new consciousness of greater breadth. Even under conditions of deprivation, disorder and stress where options may be narrowed (to put it technically), young people are still out there making rational strategies, having flexible ideas, and setting themselves goals which are as idealistic as those of other young people.

Certainly we have moved towards the everyday world and are able to set adjustment and maladjustment, beliefs, learning, self-perceptions within a clear description of social background. Demography informs development here in a way that is unique for work in the United Kingdom.

In studying the everyday lives we gain immediate meaning and do something more useful but, of course, land ourselves with a number of delicate problems. Our data are likely to be a bit rough and ready; compromises with standards of objectivity and the niceties of measurement are likely to have to be made. Problems of diplomacy and ethics also become sharper. Indeed in Ulster at the moment, one might mention that danger of physical threat also arises. Stress for both the investigator and the participants of research are likely to be involved, even in the simple discussion of recent life experiences. Encroachment on privacy takes on a special meaning. Sensitisation of young children to the finer points of inter-group hostility must be avoided at all costs.

One has the impression certainly that the work here has been informed with high standards of scientific objectivity, almost too much so . . . , but at the same time with a genuine sensitivity and appreciation of the young people's position, their problems in retaining their integrity, and indeed appreciation that co-operation with research itself may be a worry. That is an excellent first step in a psychology no longer in a social vacuum.

Before we draw some conslusions about the story of this work, it is perhaps worth considering the social context, or, to put it another way, the stereotypes that readers across the water will bring.

Compared with the rest of the United Kingdom, outsiders see Northern Ireland still as a traditional society, that collection of more or less large villages. Much of the social setting would have been true for us in the past, and some aspects still apply. By that one means also low standards of physical life — little money, poor houses, restricted work opportunities and opportunities for leisure activities. But a more traditional community maintains many positive characteristics which have been lost elsewhere; one thinks immediately of the strength of family ties and family support, and of people having a place in the community and an identification with it, instead of anonymity and anomie; these also implying freedom from the conflict and tension in others' generation gap and youth culture. Although if we think about those two, we come already to the paradoxical point that it might be no bad thing if social change were more clearly built into Northern Ireland society through the contrariness which young people so often bring. Although Northern Ireland is not wholly alien, it has critical differences that begin to make sense within a context that social psychologists can understand.

The North of Ireland has not only suffered civil disorder and terrorism but it is more tradition-directed in the Riesman (1953) sense. That implies not only that we are here employed in a cross-cultural comparison, but also in a kind of natural experiment. This need not be a clinical, cold metaphor, but suggests a social challenge that we must understand if informed interventions are to be made, if we are to engage in the business of rational change.

We can perhaps test out some current ideas about the culture of poverty, the cycle of deprivation, the meaning of truancy, the process of labelling young delinquents, but we can also begin to compare levels of maladjustment, indexes of social alienation and other signs of deviation in a stressed community, in meaningful ways.

Certainly we must beware, as Heskin warns us, in considering that in all things Ulster people, young and old, are inevitably different: a clear temptation when only an Ulster group is studied, or when outside investigators come with fixed expectations of drama. Is it not the height of paradox, then, that we now have better, wider, more repre- sentative sample evidence of school behaviour, and of deviant attitudes and adjustment from Ulster than anywhere else? And the pity is that this evidence alone is strictly limited in value. As the Harbison group point out, English data may be ten years old, and in terms of cultural influences this is the sentient life-span of the research participants!

In the second section, we have a number of careful documentations of both the physical conditions in the Province and of demographic accounts which point clearly to the stress and the resulting distress which now seem to form the tight nexus of poverty, civil disorder, terror, psychological disturbance and coping. The value of that informed social setting is surely at its height in Murray and Boal's description of residential mobility. 'Enforced movement' provides a simple and at the same time such a vivid index of one basic aspect of Belfast life. These are bald terms indeed to cover a wealth of hate, fear, misery and frustration. And here too the study of the environment of truancy suggests that, on the one hand, an interpretation in terms of the cycle of deprivation might be the first on the list — young people don't go to school much if their parents have themselves had no great education, if their houses are of a very low standard, and if there is family unemployment. On the other hand, there is always the alternative point that it need be no irrational strategy for young people to decide that a school has nothing worthwhile to offer them. This may be related to characteristics of a particular school, and the Harbison group's evidence itself points to this. The follow-up will no doubt put flesh on the bones of the evidence and answer some of our common-sense hunches. To what extent are some fifteen-year-olds out at make-shift work which is often an excellent road to later formal employment? Or, if political crimes are sometimes forms of ordinary crime, is truancy in some sense political?

Similarly the evidence from other recent research in the Province on children in care (Graham, 1979) represents the concomitants of poverty and its damage and will certainly suggest to some that the possibilities for amelioration provided by the wider propogation of family planning and abortion law reform would enable mothers to commit themselves to wanted children in a stable family setting.

The question of individual psychological disturbance in such settings is obviously highly complicated. A large-scale survey approach can have only limited use. With careful provisos levels of disturbance both personal and social are seen to be high, higher than in Glasgow, but still not as high as those reported in the London setting. This would seem to be coping indeed. At the same time, there is evidence that the troubles have concomitants in anti-social adjustment of a serious kind. And it is sobering to note that this finding is consonant in the teachers' ratings and in the self-report of the boys themselves. Whether this anti-social behaviour and outlook is a long-term adjustment or is situationally determined is clearly still open to question; and the pessimism of Frank Fee could still be countered by the evidence of

social change which Lockhart and Elliott have presented and which will
be considered again later.

Beyond demography a number of themes command attention, for
the student of Northern Ireland, for child psychologists, for social
psychologists.

Both Mercer and Bunting and Curran and fellow workers, in their
work on the central problem of the roots of political activism in
Northern Ireland and the development of deviance, find that religion
or religious affiliation are not critical. A non-obvious finding indeed.
It is the basic, ordinary socio-economic factors and political/social
attitudes that co-vary with the willingness to demonstrate, and the
expression of alienation, aggression and autism. Undoubtedly it has
been convenient for politicians to equate religion with ideology. This
both confirms the loyalty of their supporters and obviates the search
for solutions.

In partnership here are surely Lockhart and Elliott's findings of
attitude changes among Protestant and Catholic boys at Lisnevin
Training School. Differences in ideas about soldiers, the police,
paramilitary groups, and members of the other religion can be seen to
be bridged by that old liberal panacea of personal contact, even within
the highly unfavourable setting of punitive propinquity. However
modest the interpretation of this coming together of the young
delinquent's ideas is, if attitudes and constructs can change here, are
they so strongly enmeshed?

If, secondly, we consider the studies here addressed to general
problems within child psychology, we can say again that often constraints provide the best stimulus for innovation and creativity. Cairns
in his study of young children's learning of stereotype cues has been
acutely aware of the danger of he himself, inadvertently, teaching
cognitive discriminations which the children had, thankfully, not yet
learned. This is, of course, related to the wider problem of researchers
seeming to provide support for a phenomenon that they are simply
observing. (This may arise in the most conventional psycho-metric
techniques, any traditional anti-semitism scale may contain statements
for possible endorsement which would now contravene the Race
Relations Act. . .)

So Cairns has said that there are drawbacks to working with young
children. But that they can't read questionnaires, and that they must
be delicately handled is the best thing that ever happened to him. He
was constrained to innovate and create. He was forced to design his new
and highly ingenious and indirect tasks which tell us something more
about the gradual assimilation of children into the rules and customs
and adjustments of each group separately in the Ulster divide. Children
listening to stories told in different accents, selectively perceiving and

remembering; organising dynamically those lists of pre-names eventually into acknowledged Protestant and Catholic ones, has been his contribution to the methodology of socialisation study. He has suggested lively measuring indexes which have potential for development far more fruitful than yet another inventory.

The third theme of social psychologists' interest in a natural experiment leads us to consider further advantages, if one might put it that way, of the present troubles in the Province. We have unfortunately, which is a better way of putting it, the possibility to observe a (to us) new kind of law-breaker. In the same way that Norwegian deep-sea fishermen's vocation enables one to study the effects of 'normal' father-absence (Lynn and Sawrey, 1959), the new type of 'scheduled' offender lets us see the extent to which the characteristics of these delinquents is indeed different to the unstable, inadequate others who are supposedly labelled as such. Many descriptions of young people engaged in terrorism have been given — that they are simply being used by adults, that they are themselves politically conscious and committed, that they are ordinary delinquents getting in on the act. Ruth Elliott and William Lockhart's evidence is only a first step in the solution of the puzzle but it is intriguing.

The background of the young men convicted of arson, intimidation, and causing explosions is just like that of the truants and thieves; they themselves report their adjustment in the same terms, but they do not have that history of problems and distress brought to clinics and psychologists, and they are clearly more intellectually competent and better educated. One can hardly say that they do not know what they are doing, or that they have simply drifted into a new kind of 'aggro'. But then in the next study they will have to be asked to tell us more about themselves and about their goals in their own terms. In the meantime, labelling theorists have some food for thought.

This is brave work, based on objective kinds of evidence and making modest interpretation. It is not only scientifically respectable, but properly persuasive. What now, how might one best go on? There is that theme of change, that war of the myths, and the challenge of a more humanistic approach. It has been said before that psychologists here must be preoccupied with change, and I would say that that applies anywhere, for all social-personal psychology, unless anyone is happy with the status quo anywhere. Intervention, in some form, is our goal. This in no way implies the attack of human engineering. There are many paths to change, and change ultimately comes from within people, rather than from outside in any case. We might consider, for example, rational persuasion, which has nothing to do with coercion, and is not beyond freedom and dignity. . . Here often change comes simply when we see how conditions could be made more effectively fitting to agreed needs. Surely Jean Whyte's programme falls within such a category. She proposes and has tested a nursery school plan which changes competencies, and with those, changes self-identities, I think, bringing us nearer to a goal of rational self-confidence which we have always had.

Sometimes change may come by doing something as straightforward as describing, showing, uncovering the true situation. And the N.I. situation may not be as special, deviant, sensational as some observers would have us believe. Here one could cite again many of the findings of Frank Fee and of the Harbison group — which show that young people in Ulster are not as a group qualitatively different from their peers in large cities and other areas of relative deprivation, like Scotland.

Apart from its scientific or scholarly interest, this must give heart to social agents who would see their work at least as do-able as it is elsewhere, and confound those pundits who postulate a more sensational scenario, which seem to require parallel highly dramatic amelioration — like a marathon weekend in the company of Carl Rogers himself.

But in the context of uncovering, I would take especially seriously the work concerning social attitudes, personal values, and inter-personal perceptions as we have read about them in the papers of McKernan, Lockhart and Elliott and Mercer and Bunting. Their theme has surely been that of consensus of goals and of means, agreement over priorities for social action, and possibilities for change towards agreement, which reinforce those voices in the community from masses like the Peace People to lonely individuals like the amazing Dervla Murphy (*A Place Apart,* 1978), who have pointed to the communality of problem, of interest, and of many ideals. Murphy has used the poetic phrase 'the war of myths'; as social scientists we might prefer to speak again of the exposure of a false consciousness of difference and opposition. But even if we are less allied to the formulations of Marcuse (1964) we could consider such an unknown consensus in the context of Milton Rokeach's (1970b) Belief Incongruity discussion. Rokeach's now classic account of inter-group hostility is based on the idea that surprisingly stable prejudice may be based critically not particularly on race, ethnic and other structural differences, but on the fact that people 'know' that their beliefs are not shared by certain outgroups. They believe that there is belief incongruity. But the important corollary that Rokeach has been able to demonstrate is that if one checks out the question, and if one could see that there is in fact *not* belief incongruity, or at least not total incongruity, then hostility must become meaningless, be reduced, or be compartmentalised into specific areas of difference — which after all exist between all possible groups everywhere. Rokeach himself has illustrated his thesis both with anecdotal evidence — that Southern bigots have nothing against African students in Mississipi because they were not party to the Civil War — and in intrepid experiments. White job applicants at a mental hospital chose black workmates who were clearly seen to share their relevant opinions, attitudes and beliefs. Traditional hostility can be circumvented if beliefs are seen to be congruent.

Is it not paradoxical that across the so-called religious divide, there seem in fact to be critical areas of shared goals and ideals which stretch across the whole community, while the divide is between the young boys and girls. (In gender identification, then, lies another area of the traditional orientation of Northern Ireland.)

Surely we have a special responsibility for the wider dissemination of these reliable evidences of shared goals and paths to goals. (Even the 'Protestant' ethic must change its label — if Catholic youngsters espouse ambition and a sense of accomplishment more strongly than their Presbyterian peers!) The private feelings and hopes of the community's people of goodwill can only gain confidence from them. And it is further exploration of beliefs and values that should be of future concern. The presentation of this material on shared concern, and in the further discussion of specific disagreements would be itself an intervention that would help to bring political debate and indeed disagreement on to the same piecemeal and mundane footing that it has in the rest of the United Kingdom.

And further explorations brings one to the fourth point of the more humanistic approach. This has to do with the finer points of so-called scientific methodology, but also to do with the 'drawing the veil' from our research, and with negotiating with our participants.

Kurt Lewin (1948), whom I take to be the father of modern social psychology, taught us that we must look for dynamic situations to study. It is by entering a problem, a process in flux, in tension, in development, in conflict and change that we will begin to understand the social phenomena around us. Northern Ireland qualifies! But he also taught that in some sense we must *go into* the dynamic. What does that mean? It means something very simple — that we should sometimes be prepared to dismount from our high horses and just sit around, talk, listen, look, feel. I am not suggesting that we should no longer use any objective methods of enquiry — they clearly have their place, both in providing some kinds of unarguable evidence, and in giving relatively clear comparisons with the position in other places among other people (what would we do without the Rutter Scale?). But I would be willing to sacrifice some factor analyses, some Q-sorts, even some step-wise regression analyses — because I remember that they are performed on data which has an all too human source, less precise than they are. After all, so far we have little evidence of what the fullest meaning of those items so assiduously 'completed' by the young people was; we might sometimes doubt how far they understood them in the same way the sophisticated researchers did. Next time let's not speculate about catholic Freedom and Protestant Freedom — let's ask. However, beyond that I would suggest that not only the young people, but even some of the children have got something to tell us that would put life into their marks on paper. One feels sure that Mercer and Bunting's sixth formers work out their 'loose causalities' in a tighter way for themselves; that the young girls in the Catholic schools have something more to tell us about their 'disturbance'.

Now there are always two arguments against this more relaxed, and at the same time more active approach. One, that it is not relaxed, but slack, and the other, that it is not possible because one could not/ should not expect respondents to reveal themselves in this way. The argument about the softness of the evidence, and the interference from our own preoccupations is just not powerful any more. We know so much about experimenter effects, the unconscious bias in so-called objective testing, that we are just talking about different kinds of error. Indeed more humanistic evidence at least does not hide its possible biases and ad hoc assumptions — they appear for the evaluation of the reader.

In my view, we are over modest in thinking that we cannot with care and sympathy elicit important and valid ideas and feelings and histories from our informants; and that we are arrogant in believing that only our so-called instruments can elicit the truth from them.

The second point, of privacy, is one that is much harder for an outsider to argue here. It has already been mentioned under the heading of ethics. But I would argue it now by saying that a researcher with integrity, skill and empathy can encourage some respondents to tell their story. And that is all it is.

This can no longer be done on a university open day, by coming into classrooms and going out again. It means that researchers will have to participate and to engage in social exchanges. It is arduous; tedious to set up; risky in several ways. But it will have to be tried. It would be following not only the currently fashionable Oxford school of Rom Harré and his students (1978) in their negotiations with disaffected school pupils and young boys looking for a bit of 'aggro', but the recent startling work by M. Billig at the University of Birmingham on fascists. Billig here provides a model of how one might go into the theory and practice of fascism in Britain today, combining a scholarly history of the ideological precursors in the shadowy European literature and carrying out an objective content analysis of the values advocated in a carefully selected sample of member literature produced by the

National Front Party and the British Movement, with Labour and Conservative Party literature providing controls. But he then went to the study of individual reaction to these ideological invitations — not by presenting a small sample of National Front members with the Californian F Scale, evergreen as that may seem. Going behind psychometry, if you like, he took the ideas, concepts, dynamics of the Authoritarian Personality and *talked* to members about them. He discussed with them not only the appeal that the party platform had for them, their social and political goals, their current frustrations — but he also tested out their tolerance of ambiguity, their black-white perceptions, their anti-introception, their dominance/submission ambivalences. This provided a rich set of data, which advances the Californian formulation in crucial ways. Unfortunately I have had to draw my example from something as unpalatable as the National Front.

In this book we have ideas and evidence that advance our under-standing not only of the Northern Ireland problem, but of common social problems everywhere. The authors stimulate our thinking about social change, about the value of that evidence of agreement and communality, and lead us to hope that we may now have some more immediate, spontaneous negotiations with the young people. Let them speak to us more directly. In working to understand that rich evidence it will really be one of the most interesting things to be a psychologist at this juncture of history.

References

ADELSON. J. (1971) 'The political imagination of the young adolescent', *Daedalus* 100, 1013–50   2

ALLPORT, G. W. (1958) *The Nature of Prejudice* (New York: Doubleday)   12

AMIR, Y. (1969) 'Contact hypothesis in ethnic relations', *Psychological Bulletin* 71, 319–42   12

An Industrial and Occupational Profile of the Population of Northern Ireland (1978) (Belfast: F.E.A.)   6, 14

Areas of Special Social Need (1976) (Belfast: H.M.S.O.)   1, 2, 4, 5

ASHTON, D. N. and FIELD, D. (1976) *Young Workers from School to Work* (London: Hutchinson)   6

AUNGER, E. A. (1975) 'Religion and occupational class in Northern Ireland', *Economic and Social Review*, 7, 1, 1–18   6

B.A.N. Report (1978) (Belfast: Belfast Education and Library Board)   7

BARR, S. (1977) 'The effect of Northern Irish religious cues on children's category clustering' (Unpublished BSc thesis, New University of Ulster)   12

BARRITT, D. P. and CARTER, C. F. (1962) *The Northern Ireland Problem* (London: Oxford University Press)   12

BARTON, E. S., WALTON, T. and ROWE, D. (1976) 'Using grid technique with the mentally handicapped', in P. Slater (ed.) *Explorations of Intrapersonal Space*, Vol. 1 (London: Wiley)   11

Belfast Telegraph (1976) 'Gunmen leave us', 12.8.1976; 'Death threats to peace women', 16.8.1976   15

BERNSTEIN, B. (1970) 'Education and society', *New Society* 15, No. 387 26 February 1970, 344–7   13

BILL, J. M., TREW, K. J. and WILSON, J. A. (1974) *Early leaving in Northern Ireland* (Belfast: N.I.C.E.R.)   7

BILLIG, M. (1978) *Fascists* (London: Academic Press)   16

BLALOCK, H. M. (1964) *Causal Inferences in Nonexperimental Research* (New York: Norton)   15

BLANEY, R. and McKENZIE, G. (1978) 'N.I. Community Health Survey', Report to D.H.S.S. (N.I.)   1

BLAU, P. M. and DUNCAN, O. D. (1967) *The American Occupational Structure* (New York: Wiley)   6

BLUMLER, J. C. (1971) 'Ulster on the small screen', *New Society* 18, 1248–50   2

BOAL, F. W. (1974) *Social Malaise in the Belfast Urban Area* (Belfast: Northern Ireland Community Relations Commission)   2

BOAL, F. W., DOHERTY, P. and PRINGLE, D. G. (1974) *The Spatial Distribution of some Social Problems in the Belfast Urban Area* (Belfast: N.I.C.R.C.)   1, 2, 10

BOAL, F. W., POOLE, M. A., MURRAY, R., KENNEDY, S. J. (1976) 'Religious residential segregation and residential decision-making in the Belfast Urban Area' (Social Science Research Council Final Report, Grant No. HR1165 1/2)   3

BODMAN, F. (1941) 'War conditions and the mental health of the child', *British Medical Journal* 11, 486–8   2

BOGARDUS, E. S. (1925) 'Measuring social distance', *Journal of Applied Sociology* 9, 299–308

BOGARDUS, E. S. (1933) 'A social distance scale', *Sociological and Social Research* 17, 265–71   13

BOUSFIELD, W. A. (1953) 'The occurrence of clustering in the recall of randomly arranged associates', *Journal of General Psychology* 49, 229–40   12

BOWER, T. G. R. (1977) *The Perceptual World of the Child* (London: Fontana/Open Books)   16

BOWLBY, J. (1952) *Maternal Care and Mental Health* (Geneva: W.H.O.)   2

BOYLE, J. F. (1977) 'Educational attainment, occupational achievement and religion in Northern Ireland', *Economic and Social Review* 8, 2, 79–100   14

BOYLE, K., CHESNEY, R. and HADDEN, T. (1976) 'Who are the terrorists?' *New Society* 6 May, 299   10

BRAND, E. S., RUIZ, R. A. and PADILLA, A. M. (1974) 'Ethnic identification and preference', *Psychological Bulletin* 81, 860–90   12

BRIGHAM, J. C. (1971) 'Ethnic stereotypes' *Psychological Bulletin* 76, 15–38   12

British and Irish Communist Organisation (1971) *On the Democratic Validity of the Northern Ireland State* (Belfast)   2

BRUNER, J. S. (1968) *Processes of Cognitive Growth: Infancy* (Barre, Mass.: Barre Publishing)   16

BURBURY, W. M. (1941) 'Effects of evacuation and of air-raids on city children', *British Medical Journal* 11, 660–2   2

BURT, C. (1937) *The Backward Child* (London: University of London Press)   7

CAIRNS, E. (1976) 'Children's category clustering of stereotypic

Catholic and Protestant names: the influence of age' (Unpublished paper, New University of Ulster)   12

CAIRNS, E. (1977) 'An investigation of the salience for young children in Northern Ireland of adult generated stereotypic Protestant and Catholic first names' (Paper read to the London Conference of the British Psychological Society)   12

CAIRNS, E. (1978) 'Familiarity for stereotypic Catholic and Protestant names: the influence of age and segregated vs. integrated schooling' (Unpublished paper, New University of Ulster)   12

CAIRNS, E. and DURIEZ, B. (1976) 'The influence of speaker's accent on recall by Catholic and Protestant school children in Northern Ireland', *British Journal of Social and Clinical Psychology* 15, 441–2
2, 12

CAIRNS, E. and MERCER, G. W. (1977) 'Factor-analysis of adults' ratings of stereotypic Catholic and Protestant first names' (Unpublished paper, New University of Ulster)   12

CAIRNS, E., HUNTER, D. and HERRING, L. (1978) 'Young children's awareness of violence in Northern Ireland: the influence of Northern Irish television in Scotland and Northern Ireland' (Paper presented to the annual conference of the N.I. Branch of the British Psychological Society, Virginia, Co. Cavan, May 1978)   2

CARROLL, H. C. M. (1977) 'The problem of absenteeism', in H. Carroll (ed.) (1977) *Absenteeism in South Wales* (University of Swansea: Faculty of Education)   5, 9

CATTELL, R. B., EBER, H. W. and TATSUOKA, M. M. (1970) *Handbook for the Sixteen Personality Factor Questionnaire (16PF)* (Windsor, Berkshire: N.F.E.R.)   15

CAVEN, N. and HARBISON, J. (1978) 'Persistent school non-attendance: report of a survey and discussion of the links between absenteeism and various environmental factors' (Paper presented to the Northern Ireland Regional Office, British Psychological Society conference on 'Children and Young People in a Society under Stress' in Belfast, September, 1978)   2

CAZDEN, C. B. (1971) 'Evaluation of learning in preschool education: early language development', in B. S. Bloom, J. T. Hastings and G. F. Madaus (eds.) *Handbook on Formative and Summative Evaluation of Student Learning* (New York: McGraw Hill)   8

Census of Ireland for the Year 1841 (1843) (Dublin: Alexander Thom, for H.M.S.O.)   7

Census of Ireland for the Year 1851 (1855) Part 4 Report on Ages and Education (Dublin: Alexander Thom, for H.M.S.O.)   7

Census of Ireland for the year 1861 (1863) Part 2. Report and Tables on Ages and Education (Vol. 1). (Dublin: Alexander Thom for H.M.S.O.)   7

CORRIGAN, M. (1976) 'The story so far', *Peace by Peace*, October 16 (A magazine published by the Peace People, Lisburn Road, Belfast, N.I.) 15

CRAWSHAW, R. (1963) 'Reactions to a disaster', *Archives of General Psychiatry* 9, 157–62 3

CURRAN, J. D., JARDINE, E. F. and HARBISON, J. (1977) 'Personality and attitudes in Northern Ireland schoolchildren', *Irish Psychologist*, October 14

DALRYMPLE-ALFORD, E. C. (1970) 'Measurement of clustering in free recall', *Psychological Bulletin* 74, 32–4 12

DALRYMPLE-ALFORD, E. C. (1971) 'Some further observations on the measurement of clustering in free recall', *British Journal of Psychology* 62, 327–34 12

DARBY, J. (1976) *Conflict in Northern Ireland* (Dublin: Gill and MacMillan) 1, 15

DARBY, J. and MORRIS, G. (1974) *Intimidation in Housing* (Northern Ireland Community Relations Commission) 3

DARBY, J. and WILLIAMSON, A. (1978) *Violence and the Social Services in Northern Ireland* (London: Heinemann) 1

EVASON, E. (1976) *Poverty: The facts in Northern Ireland* (London: Child Poverty Action Group) 1, 2

EVASON, E. (1978) *Family Poverty in Northern Ireland* (London: Child Poverty Action Group) 1

EYSENCK, S. (1965) *Manual of the Junior EPI* (London: University of London Press) 10

Family Expenditure Survey (1977) (Belfast: H.M.S.O.) 1

FARRINGTON, D. (1978) 'Truancy, delinquency, the home and the school' (Paper presented at conference organised by Division of Criminological and Legal Psychology of the British Psychological Society at King's College, London, May 1978) 5, 9

FEATHER, N. T. (1971) 'Test-retest reliability of individual values and value systems', *Australian Journal of Psychology* 23, 201–11 13

FEE, F. (1973) 'Orthogonal transformation to hypothesised factors of different orders', *British Journal of Mathematical and Statistical Psychology* 26, 188–94 4

FEE, F. (1976) *Reading and Disturbance in Belfast Schools* (Belfast: Education and Library Board) 2, 9

FEE, F. (1977) *Working Party Report of Belfast Education and Library Board* 14

FIELDS, R. M. (1973) *A Society on the Run: A Psychology of Northern Ireland* (Harmondsworth: Penguin) 2

FIELDS, R. M. (1977) *Society under Siege: A Psychology of Northern Ireland* (Philadelphia: Temple University Press) 2

FOGELMAN, K. (1978) 'School attendance, attainment and

behaviour', *British Journal of Educational Psychology*, 48, 2, 145—158

FOGELMAN, K. and RICHARDSON, K. (1974) 'School Attendance: some results from the National Child Development Study', in B. Turner (ed.) (1974) *Truancy* (London: Ward Lock)   5

FOLEY, M. (1973) 'Report to the People of Ballymurphy', Belfast: Mimeographed paper   2

FORBES, J. K. (1945) 'The distribution of intelligence among elementary school children in Northern Ireland', *British Journal of Educational Psychology* 15, 139—45   7

FORREST, R. (1978) Personal communication   14

FRANSELLA, F. and BANNISTER, D. (1977) *A Manual for Repertory Grid Technique* (London: Academic Press)   11

FRASER, R. M. (1971a) 'Ulster's children of conflict', *New Society* 17, 630—3   2

FRASER, R. M. (1971b) 'The cost of commotion — analysis of psychiatric sequelae of 1969 Belfast riots', *British Journal of Psychiatry* 118, 257—64   2

FRASER, R. M. (1972) 'At school during guerilla war' *Special Education* 61, 6—8   2

FRASER, R. M. (1973) *Children in Conflict* (London: Martin Secker and Warburg; also Pelican Books, 1974)   2, 3, 4, 13, 14

GALLOWAY, D. (1976a) 'Persistent unjustified absence from school', *Trends in Education* 4, 22—7   5

GALLOWAY, D. (1976b) 'Size of school, socio-economic hardship, suspension rates and persistent unjustified absence from school', *British Journal of Educational Psychology* 46, 40—7   5

GELATT, H. B. (1972) 'Decision making: a conceptual framework for counselling', *Journal of Counselling Psychology* 9, 240—5   6

GINZBERG, E. (1951) *Occupational Choice* (New York: Columbia University Press)   6

GOODMAN, M. E. (1964) *Race Awareness in Young Children* (New York: Crowell-Collier)   12

GRAHAM, J. M. (1974) 'Survey of school attendance trends 1966—74 in the Belfast and North East Area', in *Report of the Interdepartmental Committee on Matters Relating to Young People* (Northern Ireland Civil Service, 1974)   5

GRAHAM, J. (1979) 'Children in care in Northern Ireland' Paper presented to conference of N.I. Branch of the British Psychological Society, Belfast

HAGEN, J. W., JONGEWARD, R. H. and KAIL, R. V. (1975) 'Cognitive perspectives on the development of memory', in H. W. Reese (ed.) *Advances in Child Development and Behaviour* (New York: Academic Press)   12

HALL, S. and JEFFERSON, T. (1977) *Resistance through Rituals* (London: Hutchinson) 16

HALSEY, A. H. (1972) *Educational Priority. Volume I EPA Problems and Policies* (London: H.M.S.O.) 8

HARBISON, J. J. M. and CAVEN, N. (1978) *Persistent School Absenteeism in Northern Ireland* (Belfast: Central Economic Service, Department of Finance) 9

HARBISON, J., JARDINE, E. F. and CURRAN, J. D. (1978) 'The use of the Jesness Inventory with Northern Ireland populations', *British Journal of Criminology*, 18 14

HARDING, J., PROSKANSKY, H., KUTNER, B. and CHEIN, I. (1969) 'Prejudice and ethnic relations', in G. Lindzer and E. Aronsen (eds) *The Handbook of Social Psychology* (2nd ed.), Vol. 5 (Cambridge, Mass.: Addison-Wesley) 12

HARRE, R. and MARSH, P. (1978) *Rules of Disorder* (London: Routledge) 16

HAVELOCK, R. (1971) *Planning for Innovation through the Dissemination and Utilisation of Knowledge* (Ann Arbor: Centre for Research and Utilisation of Knowledge) 8

Housing Condition Survey (1974) (Belfast: Housing Executive) 1

HOWE, M. J. (1977) *Television and Children* (London: New University Education) 2

HUTT, C. (1972) *Males and Females* (Harmondsworth: Penguin Books) 15

JABLONSKI, E. M. (1974) 'Free recall in children', *Psychological Bulletin* 81, 522–39 12

JAHODA, G. and HARRISON, S. (1975) 'Belfast children: some effects of a conflict environment', *Irish Journal of Psychology* 3, 1–19 2, 11, 13, 14

JARDINE, E., CURRAN, J. D. and HARBISON, J. (1978) 'Young offenders and their offences: some comparisons between Northern Ireland, England and Scotland' (Paper presented to the Northern Ireland Regional Office, British Psychological Society Conference on 'Children and Young People in a Society under Stress', Belfast, September 1978) 2, 14

JENCKS, C. (1972) *Inequality* (New York: Basic Books) 7

JENVEY, S. (1972) 'Sons and haters: Ulster youth in conflict', *New Society* 21, 125–7 2

JESNESS, C. F. (1966) *Manual of the Jesness Inventory* (Palo Alto, California) 14

JONES, J. (1972) *Prejudice and Racism* (London: Addison-Wesley) 16

JUNG, C. G. (1964) *Man and His Symbols* (New York: Doubleday) 15

KATZ, D. and BRALY, K. W. (1933) 'Racial stereotypes of one hundred college students', *Journal of Abnormal and Social Psychology* 28, 280–90   12

KATZ, P. A. (1973) 'Perception of racial cues in preschool children: a new look', *Developmental Psychology* 8, 295–9   12

KATZ, P. (1976) *Towards the Elimination of Racism* (New York: Pergamon Press)   12

KELLY, G. A. (1955) *The Psychology of Personal Constructs*, (New York: W. W. Norton)   11

KRECH, D., CRUTCHFIELD, R. S. and BALLACHEY, E. L. (1962) *Individual in Society* (New York: McGraw-Hill)   12

LENSKI, G. (1963) *The Religious Factor* (Garden City, N.U.: Doubleday)   13

LEVINE, R. A. and CAMPBELL, D. T. (1972) *Ethnocentrism: Theories of Conflict Ethnic Attitudes and Group Behaviour* (New York: John Wiley)   12

LEWIN, K. (1948) *Resolving Social Conflicts* (New York: Harper)   16

LEYTON, E. (1974) 'Opposition and integration in Ulster', *Man* (New Series) 9, 185–198   1

LIKERT, R. (1932) 'A technique for the measurement of attitudes', *Archives of Psychology* No. 140 (New York: Columbia University Press)   13

LLOYD, E. V. (1976) 'School children's ethnic attitudes towards the denominational names in Northern Ireland' (Unpublished B.Sc. thesis, New University of Ulster)   12

LOFQUIST, L. H. and DAWIS, R. V. (1969) *Adjustment to Work* (New York: Appleton-Century-Crofts)

LYNN, D. B. and SAWREY, W. L. (1959) 'The effects of father absence on Norwegian boys and girls', *Journal of Abnormal and Social Psychology* 59, 258–62   16

LYONS, H. A. (1971a) 'Psychiatric sequelae of the Belfast riots', *British Journal of Psychiatry* 118, 256–73   2, 3, 4

LYONS, H. A. (1971b) 'The psychiatric effects of civil disturbances', *World Medicine* April 21, 17–20   2

LYONS, H. A. (1972a) 'Depressive illness and aggression in Belfast', *British Medical Journal* 1, 342–4   2

LYONS, H. A. (1972b) 'Psychiatric sequelae of the Belfast riots – reply', *British Journal of Psychiatry* 120, 471   2

LYONS, H. A. (1972c) 'Riots and rioters in Belfast – demographic analysis of 1674 arrestees in a two year period', *Economic and Social Review* 3, 605–14   2

LYONS, H. A. (1973a) 'Violence in Belfast – a review of the psychological effects', *Public Health* 87, 231–8   2

LYONS, H. A. (1973b) 'Violence in Belfast — a review of the psychological effects', *Community Health* 5, 163–8   2

LYONS, H. A. (1973c) 'The psychological effects of civil disturbances on children', *Northern Teacher*, Belfast, Winter 1973, 35–8   2

LYONS, H. A. (1974a) 'The psychological effects of the civil disturbances', *Aquarius*, 11–14   2

LYONS, D. A. (1974b) 'Terrorist bombing and the psychological sequelae', *Journal of Irish Medical Association* 67, 15–19   2

LYONS, H. A. (1975) 'Legacy of violence in Northern Ireland', *International Journal Offender Therapy and Comparative Criminology* 19 (3), 292–8   2

MACKENZIE, W. J. M. (1978) *Political Identity* (Harmondsworth: Penquin Books)

McKEOWN, M. (1978) 'Education', in J. Darby and A. Williamson (eds) *Violence and the Social Services in Northern Ireland* (London: Heinemann)   3

McPHAIL, P., UNGOED-THOMAS, J. R. and CHAPMAN, H. (1972) *Moral Education in the Secondary School* (London: Longman)

Manpower Service Commission (1978) *Young People and Work* (London: H.M.S.O.)

MARCUSE, H. (1964) *One-Dimensional Man* (Boston: Beacon Press)   16

MARSH, A. (1974) 'Exploration in unorthodox political behaviour: a scale to measure "Protest Potential" ', *European Journal of Political Research* 15, 107–29   15

MERCER, G. W., BUNTING, B. and SNOOK, S. (1978) 'Northern Ireland university students contact with the civil disturbances: factor pattern and psychological correlates' (Paper presented at the Northern Ireland branch of the British Psychological Society conference, Virginia, Co Cavan, May)   15

MERCER, G. W., BUNTING, B. and SNOOK, S. (1979) 'The effects of location, experiences with the civil disturbances and religion on death anxiety and manifest anxiety in a sample of Northern Ireland University students', *British Journal of Social and Clinical Psychology*, 18, 151–158   15

MIDDLETON, M. R., TAJFEL, H. and JOHNSON, M. B. (1970) 'Cognitive and affective aspects of children's national attitudes', *British Journal of Social and Clinical Psychology* 9, 122–34   2

MILLER, R. (1978) *Attitudes to Work in Northern Ireland* (Belfast: Fair Employment Agency)   6

MILLHAM, S., BULLOCK, R. and HOSIE, K. (1978) *Locking Up Children* (London: Saxon House)   1

MILNER, D. (1975) *Children and Race* (Harmandsworth: Penguin)   12

MILNOR, A. (1976) 'Politics, violence and social change in Northern

Ireland', *Occasional Paper No. 5* (Ithaca, New York: Western Societies Program, Cornell University)　2

MOELY, B. E. and JEFFREY, W. E. (1974) 'The effect of organization training on children's free recall of category items', *Child Development* 45, 135–43　12

MONS, W. E. M. (1941) 'Air raids and the child', *Lancet* 11, 625–6　2

MOORE, D. K. (1972) 'Language research and preschool language training', in C. S. Lavatelli (ed.) *Language Training in Early Childhood Education* (Urbana, Illinois: University of Illinois Press) 8

MORRISON, L. M., WATT, J. S. and LEE, T. R. (1974) *Educational Priority Volume 5: E.P.A. – a Scottish Survey* (London: H.M.S.O.) 8

MOTT, J. (1969) *The Jesness Inventory: Application to Approved School Boys* (London: H.M.S.O.)　14

MURPHY, D. (1978) *A Place Apart* (London: John Murray)　16

MURRAY, R., BOAL, F. W. and POOLE, M. A. (1975) 'Psychology and the threatening environment', *Architectural Psychology Newsletter* 5 (4), 30–4　3

MURRAY, R. and OSBORNE, R. (1977) 'Horn Drive: a cautionary tale', *New Society* 21 April, 106–8　3

NEIMARK, E., SLOTNICK, N. S. and ULRICH, T. (1971) 'Development of memorization strategies', *Developmental Psychology* 5, 427–32　12

NIE, N., BENT, D. H. and HULL, C. H. (1970) *Statistical Package for the Social Sciences* (New York: McGraw-Hill)　13

NORRIS, M. (1977) 'Construing in a detention centre', in D. Bannister (ed.) *New Perspectives in Personal Construct Theory* (London: Academic Press)　11

Northern Ireland Household Survey (1977) (Belfast: Housing Executive)　1

O'DONNELL, E. E. (1977) *Northern Irish Stereotypes* (Dublin: College of Industrial Relations)　2

O'NEILL, P. (1978) 'A multidimensional scaling approach to the study of the development of ethnic name stereotyping in Northern Ireland' (Unpublished B.Sc. thesis, New University of Ulster)　12

Opportunities at Sixteen (1978) (Belfast: H.M.S.O.)　1

ORLEY, J. (1976) 'The use of grid technique in social anthropology', in *The Measurement of Intrapersonal Space – Volume 1: Explorations in Intrapersonal Space* (ed.) P. Slater Chichester: Wiley　11

OVERY, R. (1972) 'Children's play' *Community Forum 2*

PAYNE, J. (1974) *Educational Priority Volume 4: EPA Surveys and Statistics* London: H.M.S.O.)　8

PEAKER, J. F. (1967) 'The regression analysis of the national survey', in *Children and their Primary Schools* (London: H.M.S.O.)   7

PERRY, S. E. (1956) *The Child and his Family in Disasters*, (NAS-NRC, No. 394, Washington D.C.)   3

Persistent School Absenteeism in Northern Ireland (1978) (Central Economic Service, Department of Finance, Northern Ireland Civil Service)   5

PROSHANSKY, H. (1966) 'The Development of Intergroup attitudes', in I. W. Hoffman and M. L. Hoffman (eds) *Review of Child Development Research*, Vol. 2 (New York: Russell Sage Foundation)   12

RIESMAN, D., GLAZES, N. and DENNY, R. (1953) *The Lonely Crowd: A Study of The Changing American Character* (New York: Doubleday)   16

ROBINS, D. and COHEN, P. (1978) *Knuckle Sandwich: Growing Up in the Working-Class City* (Harmondsworth: Penguin)   16

ROBINSON, J. A. (1966) 'Category clustering in free recall' *Journal of Psychology* 62, 279–85   12

ROE, Anne (1957) 'Early determinants of vocational choice', *Journal of Counselling Psychology* 4, 212–17   6

ROGERS, S. and TITTERINGTON, J. (1978) *A Survey of Non-Accidental Injury Registers in Northern Ireland* (Belfast: Ulster College)   1

ROKEACH, M. (1969) 'Value systems in religion', *Review of Religious Research* 11, 3–23   13

ROKEACH, M. (1970a) 'Faith, hope and bigotry', *Psychology Today*, April   13

ROKEACH, M. (1970b) *Beliefs, Attitudes and Values* (San Francisco: Jossy-Bass)   16

ROKEACH, M. (1973) *The Nature of Human Values* (New York: Free Press)   13

ROSE, R. (1971) *Governing Without Consensus: An Irish Perspective* (London: Faber and Faber)   2, 13, 14

ROSE, R. (1972) 'The market for policy indicators', in A. Shonfield and S. Shaw (eds) *Social Indicators and Social Policy* (London: Heinemann)   13

RUSSELL, J. (1973) 'Violence and the Ulster schoolboy', *New Society* 25, 204–6   2

RUSSELL, J. (1975a) 'Northern Ireland: socialization into conflict', *Social Studies Irish Journal of Sociology* 4, 2   13

RUSSELL, J. (1975b) 'The sources of conflict', *The Northern Teacher*, 3–11   14

RUTTER, M. (1967) 'A children's behaviour questionnaire for completion by teachers: preliminary findings', *Journal of Child Psychology and Psychiatry* 8, 1–11   9

RUTTER, M. (1975) *Helping Troubled Children* (Harmondsworth: Penguin)   10

RUTTER, M., YULE, B., QUINTON, D., ROWLANDS, O., YULE, W. and BERGER, M. (1974) 'Attainment and adjustment in two geographical areas — III. Some factors accounting for area differences', *British Journal of Psychiatry*, 125, 520–33   4

RUTTER, M., COX, A., TUPLING, C., BERGER, M. and YULE, W. (1975) 'Attainment and adjustment in two geographical areas: I. The prevalence of psychiatric disorder', *British Journal of Psychiatry* 126, 520–533   4

RUTTER, M., TIZARD, J. and WHITMORE, K. (1970) *Education, Health and Behaviour* (London: Longman)   2, 4

SALMON, P. (1976) 'Grid measures with child subjects', in P. Slater (ed.) *Explorations of Intrapersonal Space*, Vol. 1 (London: Wiley) 11

SAUNDERS, C. R. and DAVIES, M. B. (1976) 'The validity of the Jesness Inventory with British delinquents', *British Journal of Social and Clinical Psychology* 15   14

SCHAFFER, R. (1977) *Mothering* (London: Fontana/Open Books)

SCHELLENBERG, J. A. (1977) 'Area variations in violence in Northern Ireland', *Sociological Focus* 10, 69–78   2

SCHMIDT, H. D. (1960) 'Bigotry in schoolchildren', *Commentary* 29, 253–7   2

SIEGEL, S. (1956) *Nonparametric Statistics for the Behavioural Sciences* (New York: McGraw-Hill)   13

SLATER, P. (ed.) (1977) *The Measurement of Intrapersonal Space — Volume 2: Dimensions of Intrapersonal Space* Chichester: Wiley 11

Social Trends (1977) (London: H.M.S.O.)   15

Social and Economic Trends in Northern Ireland (1978) (Belfast: H.M.S.O.)   1

SPELMAN, B. J. (1979) *Pupil Adaptation to Secondary School* (Belfast: N.I.C.E.R.)   7

SPENCER, A. E. C. W. (1974) 'Urbanization and the problem of Ireland', *Aquarius* 82–90   2

Statistics Relating to Approved Schools for the Year 1970 (1972) (London: H.M.S.O.)   10

STEWART, A. T. Q. (1977) *The Narrow Ground. Aspects of Ulster 1609–1969* (London: Faber and Faber)   15

STRINGER, M. and CAIRNS, E. (1978) 'Protestant and Catholic children's ratings of stereotyped Protestant and Catholic faces' (Paper read to Annual Conference of the British Psychological Society (N.I. Branch), Virginia)   12

STURGE, C. (1976) 'Reading retardation and anti-social behaviour', in Berger, M., Yule, W. and Rutter, M. 'Attainment and adjustment in two geographical areas', *British Journal of Psychiatry* 126, 510–19   2

Suitability of Boys for Training School (1976) (Belfast: Statistics and Economics Unit, Department of Finance)   2

SUPER, D. (1957) *The Psychology of Careers* (New York: Harper)   6

TAJFEL, H. and JAHODA, G. (1966) 'Development in children of concepts and attitudes about their own and other nations: a cross-national study', *Proceedings of the XVIIIth International Congress of Psychology* (Moscow, Symposium 36, 17–33)   2

TAJFEL, H., NEMETH, C., JAHODA, G., CAMPBELL, J. D. and JOHNSON, M. B. (1970) 'The development of children's preferences for their own country: a cross-national study', *International Journal of Psychology* 5, 245–53   2

TAYLOR, L. and NELSON, S. (1978) 'Young people and civil conflict in Northern Ireland', in *The Trouble with Being Young* (Belfast: D.H.S.S.)   1, 2, 10, 14

TENNENT, T. G. (1971) 'School non-attendance and delinquency', *Journal of Educational Research* 13, 185–90   5, 9

THURSTONE, L. L. (1931) 'The measurement of social attitudes', *Journal of Abnormal and Social Psychology* 26, 249–69   13

TREW, K. J. (1977) 'Teaching reading in the urban school; a study and its methodology', in V. Greany (ed.) *Studies in Reading* (Dublin: The Educational Co.)   7

TURNER, I. F. (1977) *Preschool Playgroups Research and Evaluation Project Final Report to D.H.S.S. (N.I.)*   8

TURNER, I. F. and WHYTE, J. (1979) *The Language Dimension* (Belfast: N.I.C.E.R.)   8

TYERMAN, M. J. (1968) *Truancy* (University of London Press)   5

UNGOED-THOMAS, J. R. (1972) 'Patterns of adolescent behaviour and relationships in Northern Ireland', *Journal of Moral Education* 2, 53–61   2, 14

VALLANCE, R. C. and FORREST, R. (1971) 'A study of the Jesness Inventory with Scottish children', *British Journal of Educational Psychology* 338–44   14

VAUGHAN, G. M. (1963) 'Concept formation and the development of ethnic awareness', *Journal of Genetic Psychology* 103, 93–103   12

VAUGHAN, G. M. (1964) 'The development of ethnic attitudes in New Zealand school children', *Genetic Psychological Monographs* 70, 135–75   12

WADESWORTH, M. E. J. (1975) 'Delinquency in a national sample of children', *British Journal of Criminology* 15   2

WARD, C. (1978) *The Child in the City* (London: Architectural Press)   16

WEBER, M. (1948) *The Protestant Ethic and the Spirit of Capitalism* (London: Allen and Unwin)　13

WEST, D. and FARRINGTON, D. (1973) *Who Becomes Delinquent* (London: Heinemann)　2, 10

WHYTE, J. (1978) 'Interpretations of the Northern Ireland problem: an appraisal', *Economic and Social Review* 9, 257–82　1, 2, 15, 16

WILSON, G. D. (1975) *Manual for the Wilson–Patterson Attitude Inventory* (Windsor, Berkshire: N.F.E.R.)　15

WILSON, J. A. (1971) *Environment and Primary Education* (Belfast: N.I.C.E.R.)　7

WILSON, J. A. and TREW, K. J. (1975) 'The Educational Priority School', *British Journal of Educational Psychology* 45, 10–19　7

WISEMAN, S. (1967) 'The Manchester Survey', in *Children and their Primary Schools* (London: H.M.S.O.)　7

ZIV, A., KRUGLANSKI, A. W. and SHULMAN, S. (1974) 'Children's psychological reactions to wartime stress', *Personality and Social Psychology* 30, 24–30　2

ZUCKERMAN, M. (1975) *Manual and Research Report for the Sensation Seeking Scale* (Newark, Delaware: University of Delaware, Psychology Department)　15

Author Index

Subject Index